PRA

MW00680566

"This book is a powerful tool for those who suffer with suicidal depression and those who care for them."

—**Jean Larch, author of *Dying to be Free***

"Jeff Elhart and Christy Buck have assembled a simple and practical approach for each of us to be engaged in saving lives and ensuring those who struggle with depression get the help they deserve. Bringing their perspectives of advocacy, lived experience, and mental health leadership to the task, their book, be nice., advances an understandable set of responses calling on each of us to notice a change in behavior, invite a conversation of love and compassion, challenge the stigma surrounding mental illness, and empower the individual to seek assistance. Something so simple can make all the difference in the world and will serve as an act of care and compassion rather than an intrusion. This book provides a helpful and useful approach to intervene when someone we care for is struggling. Sometimes, not knowing where to begin is the hard part. Jeff and Christy provide an important guide on how to take the first steps."

—**Jerry Reed, PhD, MSW, executive committee member, National Action Alliance for Suicide Prevention; senior vice president for practice leadership, Education Development Center**

"Jeff Elhart and Christy Buck have written a timely and effective tool to combat the growing epidemic of anxiety, depression, and suicide. Within these pages, you will find hope and practical steps to help yourself or someone who may be struggling."

—**Todd Mullins, senior pastor, Christ Fellowship Church**

"This book is the drizzle that will begin a downpour. We must stop the stigma of mental illness or we will not be able to serve those struggling. The stigma will be eliminated when so many stories of pain and recovery are told that honesty, receiving help, and healing are the norm. Jeff shares honestly about that pain and healing. Christy reveals a clear path for creating an environment of care.

Read this, and build a team that will reveal how individuals, families, schools, businesses, communities, and churches can be agencies of restoration. You will be empowered to be part of saving lives and to flood your community with hope."

—Jim Liske, executive director, Movement.org

"**be nice.** gently but deeply shares the authors' personal learnings from family mental health challenges and suicide. The tangible tools in the book are easy to remember and put into use, instilling confidence to ask questions and take action if we suspect someone may be at risk of suicide. I am happy to endorse this gentle, honest, and potentially life-saving book."

— David W. Covington, LPC, MBA, CEO and president, RI International (Recovery Innovations, Inc.)

"The **be nice.** action plan's key component of notice what others are experiencing opens the door to invite to have communication and challenge to make a difference. The **be nice.** action plan is the perfect program for mental health and fitness because it empowers an individual in the pursuit of their own mental health while encouraging a cultural awareness of mental health. This empowerment is needed to shape change and provide framework around suicide prevention and mental fitness."

—Eric Hipple, author of *Real Men Do Cry*, NFL quarterback, Mental Fitness Consultant, and be nice. ambassador

"Providing an easy-to-understand and informative guide to mental health issues, Buck draws on decades of professional and personal experience in making this complicated topic highly relatable for people of all ages, while Elhart honestly shares pain and grief from the loss of his brother with his heart-wrenching storytelling. The creation of this book by this dynamic duo will improve, change, and save lives. It is a must-read."

—Terri DeBoer, meteorologist, WOOD TV | WOTV | WXSP

"Schools need mental health awareness and strong suicide prevention programs more than ever for our students and adult populations. The **be nice.** action plan provides schools with the tools and roadmap to establish a strong system of support from a macro level right down to the needs of every individual. It is easy to follow and highly impactful when helping all students and staff reach their fullest potential!"

—**Roger Bearup, superintendent of Grandville Public Schools, Grandville, Michigan**

"The **be nice.** action plan is an all-encompassing suicide prevention initiative that enhances the work of school professionals. We have seen the impact of **be nice.** at Zeeland Public Schools with our students, staff, and community. **be nice.** supports mental health education, prevention, and intervention. It is also a macro-level movement that increases awareness of brain health while reducing the stigma associated with mental health. This systemic response can be customized to your setting and change the culture of your school, business, faith-based organization, and community. Through the work of the Mental Health Foundation and the **be nice.** Initiative, we can all become part of the solution and make our schools, organizations, and communities suicide-safe places to live, work, and play. If there was ever a time to be serious about our mental health, it is now!"

—**Todd Kamstra, MSW, Zeeland Public Schools high school student success coordinator**

"Christy Buck and Jeff Elhart have written an invaluable resource that churches who are serious about ministering to all their congregants, including suicidal congregants, can use. Their goal is a 'sensible and accessible tool' for churches who are implementing a culture of suicide prevention, and they are successful. They explain with clarity the **be nice.** action plan and **be nice.** faith. They use regular language with clear examples from everyday life, including their own powerful stories. A church using this resource will be prepared to save lives. What is more, their call to action makes clear that suicide prevention is everyone's job. Churches serious about suicide prevention must keep this resource at their fingertips."

—**Karen Mason, PhD, professor of counseling and psychology at Gordon-Conwell Theological Seminar, author of *Preventing Suicide: A Handbook for Pastors, Chaplains and Pastoral Counselors* and coauthor of *Preaching Hope in Darkness: Help for Pastors in Addressing Suicide from the Pulpit***

"Honest. Accurate. Accessible. Jeff Elhart and Christy Buck have created an outstanding resource for individuals and families grappling with suicide. **be nice.** includes accurate information and resources useful to individuals with suicidal thinking, friends and family members, and for community organizers and advocates. Numerous examples of honest reckoning with suicide in a family and in our communities are provided. The information is accurate and is presented clearly so that it is accessible and relatable. Suicide is common and is often hidden. This work brings great light and hope to the many who live with the impact of suicide. Together we can take more notice, invite persons into helpful dialogs, challenge the myths, and empower individuals to engage in a path of healing. Read it!"

—Anita Everett, MD, DFAPA, director, Center for Mental Health Services US, HHS Substance Abuse and Mental Health Services

"Christy Buck and Jeff Elhart's new book, **be nice.**: 4 Simple Steps to Recognize Depress and Prevent Suicide, takes a simple yet ingenious way to help individuals and organizations learn tools focused on improving mental health and well-being, including preventing suicide. Together, they successfully blend suicide- and mental health-focused research with lived experience to educate the reader about the **be nice.** action plan. The simplicity of the be nice. plan is that it can be easily learned and integrated into broader, multidimensional, and comprehensive suicide prevention programs at home, work, and in the community. Using an upstream approach, the authors empower the reader to learn techniques to improve observation and communication skills and to demonstrate daily compassion, caring, and empathy. These skills help to form the foundation for a better world—one in which all of us, and the people we care about, will benefit from meaningful human connection, stronger relationships, and overall higher quality of life."

—Jodi Jacobson Frey, PhD, LCSW-C, CEAP, professor, University of Maryland School of Social Work; chair, Social Work in the Workplace & Employee Assistance Sub-specialization; cochair, Workplace Suicide Prevention & Postvention Committee, American Association of Suicidology; chair, Financial Social Work Initiative; co-editor in chief, Journal of Workplace Behavioral Health; cofounder, International Employee Assistance Digital Archive

"From a mix of personal loss, renewal, and wisdom, Jeff Elhart and Christy Buck have created a useful and practical resource for schools, communities, families, and congregations. **be nice.** *(notice, invite, challenge, and empower) is the kind of memorable and useful guidance for mental health situations that "stop, drop, and roll" provides for fires. And at a time when mental health concerns are epidemic and exacerbated by the isolation brought on by COVID-19, it could not be more timely. This book is easy to read, share, and use. It fills the need for those times when we wonder, "They don't seem quite right . . . but what can I do?"*

—Dr. Michael F. Hogan, PhD, chairman, Hogan Health Solutions;
President George W. Bush President's Commission on Mental Health;
National Action Alliance for Suicide Prevention Executive Committee

"As evaluators of the be nice. program in West Michigan schools, our endorsement of be nice.: 4 Simple Steps to Recognize Depression and Prevent Suicide is based on our professional, firsthand knowledge of the school evaluation research data, firsthand knowledge of the lives it has changed, and personal connection with the authors and their stories. This book links the authors' family tragedies with a program designed to help others avoid similar situations. Following our evaluation of the **be nice.** *program in West Michigan schools, the Mental Health Foundation of West Michigan built upon the adaptability of this program by developing be nice. business, be nice. faith, and be nice. community. We highly endorse this book and the lifesaving value it brings to any community or organization."*

—Raymond J. Higbea, PhD, associate professor of health administration,
and director, School of Public, Nonprofit, and Health Administration,
Grand Valley State University; Rosemary Cleveland, EdD, director,
College of Education Graduate Certificate Program,
Grand Valley State University

"There are a number of pressures many people face in everyday life, and in this day and age, social media and other social stresses can create additional challenges. Those that are not facing struggles are likely to know someone who needs help, but they don't feel equipped to do so. Jeff Elhart and Christy Buck's **be nice.** *book equips readers and communities with the tools to help create hope and ultimately save lives."*

—Bill Huizenga, United States congressman

"As a keynote speaker, trainer, and consultant, I'm often asked for resources on suicide prevention for everyday people. Jeff and Christy's book *be nice.* offers so many helpful features! First, the lived experience perspective lets the reader know that the authors have walked the path—this is not just an academic curiosity. Their storytelling brings the concepts to life. Second, their bio-psycho-social approach is holistic and lets people know that many solutions exist for people experiencing suicidal intensity. Finally, their 'BE NICE' tool guides people on action steps they can take to save lives."

—Sally Spencer-Thomas, PsyD, keynote speaker,
www.SallySpencerThomas.com

Always,

be nice.®

Christy Br

be nice.®

4 SIMPLE STEPS
TO RECOGNIZE DEPRESSION AND PREVENT SUICIDE

CHRISTY BUCK, LBSW
JEFF ELHART

propermedia

Mental Health Foundation of West Michigan
349 Division Ave S.
Grand Rapids, MI 49503

© 2021 **be nice.** 4 Simple Steps to Recognize Depression and Prevent Suicide
Paperback ISBN: 978-1-7372415-0-8
E-book ISBN: 978-1-7372415-1-5

Disclaimer:
The **be nice.** action plan and its steps to notice, invite, challenge, and empower are effective steps to helping yourself or someone who is experiencing a mental health concern or crisis. This action plan is by no means a replacement for appropriate medical care or professional help. This tool is to be used as a means to aid in the process of bettering an individual's mental health or decreasing a person's risk for suicide. This book is not a tool to diagnose yourself or someone with a mental illness. When used appropriately this tool has been proven to reduce behavioral referrals and increase a person's likelihood to seek help concerning their mental health. It is also proven to aid as a positive culture shift when it comes to mental health and the way we treat others.

Mention of specific companies, organizations, or authorities in this book does not imply endorsement by the author or publisher, nor does mention of specific companies, organizations, or authorities imply they endorse this book, its author, or publisher.

MHF/be nice. Staff - text and design
John Corriveau - photograph of authors
Chip Brown - Proper Media for editorial, design and supply chain
Chris Tiegreen - editorial

First edition: 2021
10 9 8 7 6 5 4 3 2

Printed in the United States of America.

Ordering information: info@benice.org
www.benicebook.org

Meet Wayne Jeffery Elhart

This man was successful, funny, and a joy to know.

It's hard to imagine that anyone would take their own life.

If you wonder,

Why would this man take his own life?,

YOU ARE NOT ALONE.

The truth is, suicide is reality for many people—people

you may know.

And . . . the pain and grief of those who are left behind is devastating.

This book is dedicated to the memory of Wayne Jeffery Elhart and

others who have died by suicide.

May your reading provide you the tools to

HELP OTHERS WITH MENTAL ILLNESS AND PREVENT SUICIDE.

Meet the Authors

Christy Buck, LBSW
Executive Director
Mental Health Foundation of
West Michigan

Jeff Elhart
Playground Director II
Elhart Automotive Campus

The **be nice.** program and its action plan were created under Christy's leadership by the Mental Health Foundation in 2010. In 2015, the trajectory of the **be nice.** program changed the day the Elhart family reached out. Jeff Elhart called the MHF office in search of a resource at a mental health event he was hosting.

Since June 2015, together Christy and Jeff have worked tirelessly to impact a community by educating people of all genders, races, and socioeconomic classes on mental illness awareness and suicide prevention. Christy's trademarked **be nice.** program and Jeff's per-

sonal ambition to bring about change in this growing epidemic of depression and suicide has made for what has been a very passionate
and ambitious pair in equipping communities with a culture that can
improve and even save lives through a simple action plan . . . **be nice.**

Alongside of Christy and Jeff is an army of warriors helping to
win this battle. The staff of Christy's organization, volunteers, and
the community supporters for both foundations; the Mental Health
Foundation of West Michigan; and the Wayne Elhart **be nice.**
Memorial Fund have made a significant positive culture around this
topic, reduced stigma, and equipped people to administer the "stop,
drop, and roll" for those with mental illness and suicidal ideation.

This book shares the many years of professional experience in this
field by Christy and the firsthand experience of a suicide loss survivor in
Jeff. You'll find in the table of contents who authored each part as well
as a reminder at the beginning of each chapter. While the authors
are noted for your clarification, the content is a collaboration of their
experience and passion for **be nice.**

Christy Buck has passionately led the Mental Health Foundation of
West Michigan (MHF) for thirty-five years. Under her leadership, the
MHF has grown and stabilized—from a simple "pass through" grant
fund for individuals with mental illness to a multi-program, dynamic
organization. Today the MHF has a leadership role in the community
when it comes to creating awareness surrounding mental illness and
suicide prevention. This is done through two programs Christy founded, Live Laugh Love and **be nice.**®, and through the national programs

Mental Health First Aid (MHFA), Question, Persuade, Refer (QPR), and Signs Of Suicide (SOS), and Acknowledge, Care, Tell (ACT).

MHF programs provide continuous education of mental illness awareness and suicide prevention education to almost 150,000 K-12 students each year throughout Michigan with the near-term strategic goal of making its scientific, evidence-based programming available nationally by 2022. The **be nice.** program is embraced by not only school students, parents, teachers, counselors, and administration but also small to large companies and houses of worship. Christy serves as a trustee on the Grandville Public School Board; is recognized as a leader in the community for mental health, suicide prevention, and stigma reduction; and has served on many task forces and committees. Within her Holy Trinity Greek Orthodox Church community, she has served as the youth advisor and instructed Religious Education for more than thirty years.

Jeff Elhart has worked in the automobile business his entire career since the age of twelve. Along with his brother Wayne and father Kenneth, they successfully served the West Michigan community in offering sales and service of cars and trucks at their automobile dealerships. Having received many business and community recognition awards, the Elhart Automotive Campus continues serving its community under Jeff's leadership since his father's retirement in 1990 and his brother's retirement in 2010.

Since his brother's death from depression by suicide on March 27, 2015, he has become an advocate for mental illness awareness and suicide prevention. Jeff is a trained educational liaison for the Mental Health Foundation of West Michigan's **be nice.** program and has served on the MHF board as chairman and current immediate past chairman. His company supports the MHF's mission and was the first business to implement the **be nice.** program. Jeff serves on the executive committee of the National Action Alliance for Suicide Prevention and serves on two task force committees: the Faith Community Task Force and the Workplace Task Force. He has served in numerous leadership positions in his Christian life by serving the churches where he has been a member. Jeff frequently speaks on the topic of mental illness awareness and suicide prevention in his industry of the automobile business as well as other organizations including faith communities and others.

Meet the Beneficiaries

**Mental Health
Foundation of
West Michigan**

**Wayne Elhart
be nice.
Memorial Fund**

The Mental Health Foundation of West Michigan brings awareness of mental health and tools for suicide prevention to people of all ages, through the **be nice. action plan**. At the Mental Health Foundation, we believe in creating communities that recognize, understand, accept, and take action when it comes to mental health and suicide prevention. As a nonprofit organization our work is made possible by donations from everyday people who recognize the profound impact these tools can have in one's own life and the lives of others.

Help us to strengthen our communities by decreasing stigma and equipping people with tools of the action plan. Join the community of people across our country who have taken the pledge and helped to fund the Mental Health Foundation at www.benice.org.

All net proceeds from the sale of this book are split equally between the two nonprofit 501(c)(3) organizations responsible for making this book possible: the Mental Health Foundation of West

Michigan, 349 Division South, Grand Rapids, Michigan 49503; and the Wayne Elhart be nice. Memorial Fund c/o the Community Foundation of the Holland/Zeeland Area, 85 E. 8th Street, Holland, Michigan 49423.

Contents

Foreword xv

Preface xvii

Part One: Do not blame yourself as it was me.. 1

Recognizing Risks, Seeing the Signs, Saving Lives

Chapter 1: Who Would Have Known? 3

Chapter 2: Dying Wishes Granted 14

Part Two: This depression has gotten the best of me.......................... 23

Myths and Understandings

Chapter 3: Understanding Mental Illness and Suicide........................ 27

Chapter 4: Nobody Is Immune 39

Chapter 5: Dispelling the Myths... 52

Part Three: Please use my illness to help others. 65

The be nice. Action Plan

Chapter 6: A Program and an Action Plan 68

Chapter 7: notice.. 78

Chapter 8: invite... 90

Chapter 9: challenge 100

Chapter 10: empower.. 108

Part Four: God, please use me to help others. 119

A Time for Action

Chapter 11: be nice. in Action.. 122

Chapter 12: Changing the Culture with be nice. 140

Chapter 13: Saving Lives with be nice. 153

Chapter 14: Managing Your Mental Health 162

Exercises: Put be nice. into Action for Your Family............................ 172

Epilogues 181

Appendices

Appendix A: be nice. Testimonials 186

Appendix B: How to Deal with How You Feel 189

Appendix C: Glossary of Mental Illness and Suicide 192

Appendix D: If You're Feeling Suicidal Right Now 197

Acknowledgments... 202

Foreword

Written by Christy Buck

My name is Christy Buck, and I am the executive director of the Mental Health Foundation of West Michigan (MHF) and the founder of be nice. The **be nice.** program and its action plan were created by the MHF staff in 2010. Since then, the program has expanded into schools, businesses, places of worship, and community organizations across our state and country.

To learn the **be nice.** action plan is to learn four simple steps that can provide an individual with knowledge surrounding mental health and illness and gain the confidence to take action every day and in crisis situations.

It is our hope that after reading this book you will have a greater understanding of mental health, mental illness, suicide, and how the be nice. action plan can be used as a tool to have open and educated conversations about mental health and suicide risk. It is our mission to equip people with the knowledge to recognize, understand, accept, and take action when it comes to mental health.

Three decades of experience tell me that changing the climate of a school, workplace, or community regarding mental health begins with individuals. We are never too young or too old to start talking about mental health and the be nice. action plan. We can ultimately save lives by doing so. Thank you for investing your time and effort in making a change in yourself and your community.

Preface

Written by Wayne Elhart

Kathy, family & friends

I love you all.

This depression has gotten the best of me.

Do not blame yourself as it was me.

Please use my illness to help others ~~in my~~

God please help me to help others.

Wayne

PART ONE

Do not blame yourself as it was me.

Recognizing Risks,
Seeing the Signs,
Saving Lives

PART ONE

Do not blame yourself as it was me.

*Recognizing Risks,
Seeing the Signs,
Saving Lives*

You are about to read an account of Wayne's journey with depression. This story or a story like it may be totally foreign to you. If so, that's good news. It may, however, sound familiar to some of you as you may have experienced a similar tragedy in your personal life. Either way, I am sharing Wayne's story as it provides a roadmap of how many of us who struggle with a mental illness, mostly depression, can face dire thoughts and even take unbelievable action up to and including suicide. This book will provide you an action plan in just four simple steps to help others win the fight against this growing epidemic of depression and suicide.

Who Would Have Known?

Written by Jeff Elhart

It was the summer of 2010 when my cell phone registered an unexpected text message: "I love you."

My brother was fifty-six at the time. Not knowing how to deal with his message, I meditated on it for the day. My mind was churning. Was it sent by him? Was he just saying thank you for my attempt to help him in his struggling time? Or did this mean Wayne was saying goodbye?

Playground Director

Sometime during the late 1990s, Wayne created new titles for his staff and himself. Everyone at Elhart Pontiac GMC Jeep, Inc. carried the title of CEO–Customer Relations. He gave himself the title of Playground Director.

Before his retirement in 2010, Wayne and I were partners in our family business, Elhart Automotive Campus in Holland, Michigan. The business, established in 1965 by our parents, Ken and Barbara Elhart, offers several brands: GMC Trucks, Nissan, Hyundai, Genesis, and Kia. We offered Pontiac, Jeep, and Dodge for most of those first fifty-five years, up to the time of the General Motors and Chrysler bankruptcy in 2009.

Wayne's directive to his staff was to treat the customer the way they would want to be treated. If they as a staff member had to make a decision to make sure that the customer experience was exceptional, then they were to do it. After all, they were the CEO of customer relations!

Being the Playground Director meant to Wayne that everyone at the dealership was there to work hard and play hard. If a situation came up on the playground of the dealership, Wayne would step in. That didn't happen often, but when it did, Wayne would use some directives after giving his playmates every opportunity to do the right thing. He might say, "This is my way or the highway," or, "Maybe you would be suited better somewhere else," or, "I didn't notice your name on the sign out front." Years later, even his terminated employees respected him for his forthrightness. Wayne didn't sugarcoat anything. You could take what he said to the bank.

You could count on Wayne. He provided the strength of leading from the top. He honored those who worked hard and rewarded them with opportunities to play hard. Through his ability to corral the troops on the playground, he was able to build and maintain a strong family atmosphere at work, at home, and with those he mentored.

Traveling the Road to the Bottom

Like the mountain passes in the Rockies, life's journey is not a straight or level road. That was the experience for most business owners and the American public during the financial recession of 2008 to 2010.

It was no different for Wayne, except he faced it head on with the gifts God had given him. Wayne lived the fruits of the Spirit: love, joy, peace, forbearance, kindness, goodness, faithfulness, gentleness, and self-control. He used these gifts to lift the spirits of others around him—his family, his employees, his friends, and those he mentored.

Despite Wayne's gift of sharing good cheer, he was not protected from hardship. The turmoil of the auto industry crisis in 2009 to 2010 created an environment he couldn't run from but had to face head on.

The journey of maneuvering through the bankruptcies of General Motors and Chrysler may have built character that Wayne already possessed, but it was the news of March 2010 that triggered his depression.

As a result of the phone call from a General Motors executive, once a close business associate, the wind went out of Wayne's sails. The plans for our business under General Motors' reorganization took a 180-degree turn. Everything our family business had planned for was being overturned by the federal government.

If there was a tipping point in Wayne's life, this was it. Though he spoke with strength to his family, he was moving quickly into depression.

Noticeable Changes in Wayne

My wife, Cherie, and I took many walks down the Lake Michigan shoreline talking about Wayne during the early summer that year, 2010. We talked about Wayne's weight loss—thirty-plus pounds and noticeably leaner. We noticed his thinner face and gray complexion. I know his coworkers and friends noticed too.

Wayne was losing his positive attitude and outlook. He was having trouble making decisions and deferred many personnel decisions to me or at least asked what should be done. His normally confident nature was gone.

Wayne was drowning in his depression. It was fueled by fear of not being able to continue his family business and provide employment for his employees, many of whom had stood by him for decades. Wayne was a humble man who rarely expressed anger, but it still haunted him. He was angry at the government's interference with General Motors' reorganization plan. The sky was falling into his world. He wanted out.

My Own Journey with Depression

I had had my own bout with depression ten years earlier. It was triggered by guilt. In 2000, I released (okay, fired) a key employee who had worked with our family business for twenty-seven years. I've never been through a divorce, but that's the only way I can describe my pain at the time. Working with this employee, with all the successes and challenges we experienced together, was unforgettable. I couldn't just turn off the memories. My guilt turned into sadness. The good news is that I searched out a fix and learned that my sadness was depression.

When my doctor asked if anyone else in my family dealt with depression, I said my mother did. At the time, I didn't realize the degree with which she had been battling the illness so didn't think much of it. I was just sad. I couldn't sleep. I couldn't get the guilt off my mind. A swirling feeling of downward pressure was new to me. My journey with depression lasted for several years, and the first was quite severe; I had to keep my mind occupied at all times or it would wander off to, "Why did I do that?" I beat myself up countless times and was losing my confidence at home and at work. The only person I told of my illness was Cherie. I hid it—or at least think I did—from everyone else.

My doctor prescribed an antidepressant and told me it might take thirty-sixty days to feel the effect. Anxious and losing patience, I later called to see if a stronger dose would be acceptable. He doubled my dosage after about thirty days.

Time went on, and the hurt from the guilt continued. Between time and Zoloft, however, my mind was beginning to feel some ease from the constant pain. In about a year, I felt I was capable of living with the decision I had made, and it was time to slowly remove myself from the drug (with my doctor's assurance)—but I still held on to that nagging guilt.

Throwing Life-Rings

Having felt the effects of depression myself, I shared with Cherie that Wayne needed some help. I figured that if an antidepressant helped me, it could help him too. After all, we were brothers; we must have at least some of the same DNA. So one day in June 2010, I spoke to Wayne about seeing his doctor, who also happened to be mine. He said he would make the call to set up an appointment, but I sensed it was time to empower myself to make sure he did. I picked up the phone in his office, dialed our doctor, and handed the phone to Wayne. He made his appointment. Relieved that he was able to see the doctor that week, I felt we were one step closer to helping him overcome his depression.

The Text

That's when his text came. "I love you." Between June and July 2010, Wayne had isolated himself, lost his confidence and a lot of weight, felt hopeless and helpless, and had difficulty getting out of bed. Sleeping through the night was not even in the picture. He was trying to hang on to a few life-rings thrown his way, but life was spiraling out of control.

Did the text mean he was thanking me for trying to help him? Or did it mean he was saying goodbye? I didn't know.

I also didn't know what to do with the text. Should I tell anyone about it? Was it real? Did it actually come from Wayne's fingers and from his phone?

I let it pass—for now.

A Time for Transition

The summer of 2010 goes down as a record of walks along the beach for Cherie and me. Dealing with our business turmoil and trying to help Wayne with his emotional strain, we leaned on God's beauty for motivation and discernment in our quest for solutions. Remembering that Wayne wanted to retire at fifty-five, Cherie suggested it might be a good time to consider the business transition, since Wayne was now fifty-six. We agreed to sleep on it.

I asked the question later that week. "Wayne, I know you wanted to retire at fifty-five. You're fifty-six now. Business is a challenge and not fun for you anymore. Is it time for our transition? I'd rather remain partners, but maybe it's worth considering."

I told him I wasn't sure if I had the funds to buy his half of the business, and he didn't know if he would have enough to live on in retirement. We decided to think about it for a couple of weeks, talk it over with our wives, and do due diligence with our attorney and accountant. During that time, I reached out to my uncle George, who had experience in the mental illness treatment industry. I told him what Wayne and I were considering, and George surprised me with his comments.

"I retired a few years ago, and I have to tell you my story. I was fine for about ninety days, but then I became bored with nothing to do. I felt worthless. I became depressed. I received some help and medication, and now I'm okay." But he went on to offer an important piece of advice to give to Wayne. "You have to make sure you have something to run to and not from when you choose to retire."

I thought that advice was perfect coming from a respected relative, so I asked George to meet with Wayne and his wife, Kathy, to have the same conversation. He agreed and talked with them the next week.

Wayne approached me in July and said he wanted to pursue the thought of the business transition. He was convinced he had enough to look forward to in retirement and felt ready for this change. But was he?

On the last day of 2010, Cherie and I purchased Wayne and Kathy's half of the business. And for the next three and a half years until the summer of 2014, Wayne enjoyed life tremendously. He did the things he loved to do—skiing in the winter in Colorado and boating in Lake Michigan and Lake Huron during the summer. Wayne never saw a bluebird day in Colorado that he didn't ski at least twenty-five thousand vertical feet. One year he logged more than 1.3 million vertical feet over fifty-nine days! Later that summer, he traveled hundreds of miles and spent more than sixty days on our shared boat.

Wayne was a social butterfly. With his words, smile, and quick wit, he could bring an audience to their hands and knees, aching with laughter. He was a mentor to many, including those at our business and many other young men who are now successful businessmen in their respective fields. Many of them thought of Wayne as a second father.

But in 2014, he quit doing most of the things he enjoyed. He went the whole summer without putting his boat in the water. He didn't spend time on our family boat. He made no plans for skiing. He isolated himself again and was clearly depressed.

One September day, I asked Wayne how his summer had gone without boating. When he said one of his two dogs was sick and he felt he should stay home, I believed him. He and Kathy had no children, and I knew he cared a lot about those dogs. But I still knew he was depressed.

It was difficult to see, but I noticed that something more was needed than my shallow talks with him. Wayne's complexion was so white, and he looked so scared. I had Wayne call his doctor to set up an appointment for later that day. His doctor prescribed for him the same antidepressant that I was on. I thought that was the fix. In time, Wayne would be back to himself.

Just as I had been impatient with the results with my medication for depression, Wayne was feeling the same anxiety. His patience was running thin. He was getting thinner, now down forty pounds. Though Wayne lived the fruits of the Spirit apart from attending a church, I knew medication of the brain was only one tool to help him. Another one would be faith.

It was just a few short months later that Cherie and I invited Wayne and Kathy to Florida to stay a few days with us. When in Florida, we attend Christ Fellowship, a large church in Palm Beach Gardens, so we all attended the weekend of December 7, 2014. The pastor spoke from Isaiah 43:2: "I will be with you; and when you pass through the rivers, they will not sweep over you. When you walk through the fire, you will not be burned; the flames will not set you ablaze." The pastor asked those who were struggling with inner demons to raise their hands and he would pray over them to receive Jesus as their Lord and Savior and ultimate healer of their troubles. Wayne's hand shot up like a rocket! The Holy Spirit was at work. Wayne received Jesus Christ as his Lord and Savior. He had been baptized in the Methodist Church as a youngster but did not have Jesus in his heart for decades and had not been involved in the church or spent time in the Bible. But from that day forward, Wayne was in the Word each and every day, seeking God's support for his struggles and looking for help in releasing the demons from his mind.

Just a few weeks later, Wayne said, "Jeff, look what I found!" He was holding a Bible.

"Where did you find this?" I asked.

"Look inside the cover," he said.

I did. It was the King James Version of the Bible he received from our First United Methodist Church when he graduated from third grade Sunday School. "Wow, Wayne, that is so cool!"

"Yeah! I'm through Genesis already! There are a lot of thees and thous in there!"

His energy—and his sense of humor—seemed to be returning.

While Wayne was showing some strength from his faith and medication, he was still distant from others and not like himself. I just so happened to be reading my favorite pastor Rick Warren's Daily Hope Devotional on January 19, 2015 when I thought I'd discovered the answer to Wayne's troubles. Rick spoke that day about "how to deal with how you feel."[1] Rick Warren and his wife, Kay, became suicide loss survivors after they lost their son Matthew on April 6, 2013, at the age of twenty-seven to a lifelong illness of depression.

Especially since their loss, Pastor Warren's messages frequently provide hope for those in our society who struggle with depression. Rick suggested that if you're struggling with your emotions, you're struggling with one of two emotions: worry/fear or anger. He suggested to determine which emotion it is, then define what you're afraid of or angry about. Then ask yourself if what you're feeling is true or not.

I thought Wayne was dealing with fear, primarily that he would run out of money. So I shared this devotional with him. I was right. He was afraid of running out of money. Were his perceptions right, or were those fears exaggerated—as fears often are? The best way to explore the truth of that fear was to have him meet with his accountant. He and Kathy did that a couple of weeks later, and it

---

[1] See Appendix B for a summary of this message.

turned out that he was in great financial shape. He could put that fear behind him. I thought that was the fix.

It wasn't. It wasn't enough. I found Wayne dead on March 27, 2015.

chapter

2

Dying Wishes Granted

Written by Jeff Elhart

Wayne's battle with major depression had been relatively short, but it was much more intense than any of us knew. I and the rest of the family were shocked, and I wasn't sure what to do next or even what to think. Wayne and I had spent so much of life together—brothers, best friends, partners in business for more than three decades. I didn't know how to process what had happened. Once I got past the initial shock, the question of "why" kept coming up in my mind. And I didn't have any answers for it.

I had plenty of emotions, though. Survivors of suicide go through a wide range of feelings, and many experience anger or guilt, or a combination of the two. I knew I wasn't angry at Wayne, and I really didn't have any anger toward God for what had happened. But I experienced a lot of guilt. I had some deep battles with all the questions I had, particularly what I might have done differently to help Wayne before it was too late. How had I not noticed how much he was struggling? And if I had noticed, what would I have done? Why didn't I think to help him more than I did—to make sure everything was okay, even after his financial fears were settled? What else could I have done to prevent this horrible tragedy? I was glad I had done some things to help—I had gotten him to his primary care physician and helped him rediscover faith in God. But that hadn't been enough. At the time we had not found the note he had left behind to fill any of the gaps for us. What had he been thinking? Why hadn't he reached out more? All these questions kept nagging at me, and they kept me up at night.

I Had to Come Up with a Fix

Because I felt such a sense of mission from Wayne's death, I dove into research. I consumed all kinds of books and resources about depression and suicide. I learned a lot, but nothing struck me as something I could use to equip everyday people in a meaningful way. But the underlying theme was consistent. Depression is not rocket science. Preventing suicide is not Superman work. Anybody and everybody can recognize the warning signs of depression and help the person get professional help or treatment before it's too late. But I quickly learned that it is up to the loved one, coworker, or anyone who connects with regularly with the person struggling with depression who needs to provide the help.

I decided to be very intentional about coming up with a fix. A few weeks after Wayne's death, Cherie and I went back to Florida to get away but most importantly visit the pastor who helped bring Wayne back into his relationship with God. The pastor said, "Oh my goodness, you need to come back to Christ Fellowship Church to see a new movie, *Hope Bridge*, we're showing! It's about depression and suicide.

In fact, the movie producer was one of our worship leaders here not long ago. She and her husband now live in Cincinnati and have had an experience like yours. Come to the movie and meet them—David and Christie Eaton."

The movie, *Hope Bridge*, is about a high school boy who loses his father to suicide and goes on a mission to find out why. In his journey, he deals with anger, which grows to the point that he is ready to take his own life. After his counselor talks him off the ledge of a bridge, the counselor says, "It's not the pain that you're feeling. It's the fear of the pain that you're feeling."

At the end of the movie, the boy takes the reminders of his anger and burns them in his family's backyard. Then, with his mother and sister, he spreads those ashes around a new tree planted in the yard in his dad's memory.

This scene prompted me to take action with my guilt. I wrote down eleven specific situations in which, in my mind, I could have done something to help Wayne and did not. Two months after his death, we held a memorial service on Wayne's birthday by a flagpole on our dealership property. We buried part of Wayne's remains in an urn next to the flagpole. I wrote a letter to Wayne, attached the eleven situations, and inserted it into the urn. At that moment, I felt myself lifted off the ground with God's hands. I have been rid of 80 percent of the guilt I suffered with.

When we brought *Hope Bridge* to our church and community in Michigan, I invited about twenty organizations to participate by having a booth outside the sanctuary so they could provide resources on mental health, counseling, and more. I reached out to the Mental

Health Foundation of West Michigan to participate and spoke to Christy Buck, whom I had never met before.

"I need to come out and meet you!" she said.

When we met for the first time, I told her I was looking for a simple tool to help people understand the warning signs of depression and how to help those who are depressed before a life is lost. I had been trying to come up with something with the word *depression* as an acronym. Cherie had told me, "You need something simple, like 'stop, drop, and roll.'" I knew she was right. When Christy told me about be nice., forming an acrostic with the word *nice*—**notice, invite, challenge, empower**—I knew that was it. I found the fix.

"At its most basic," Christy said, "**be nice.** is a four-step action plan to notice, invite, challenge, and empower people to take action when they or someone they know may be experiencing a change in their mental health. Take it a step further, and **be nice.** becomes an upstream program that uses the action plan as a basis for mental health and suicide prevention education in schools, workplaces, places of worship, and communities as a whole."

Yes, this was it! One of my biggest prayers in my life was answered on June 29, 2015, just ninety days after Wayne's death. I found the tool to help others with the illness of depression and a tool to educate people, all people, on how to save a life from suicide. **be nice.** is the "stop, drop, and roll" for mental illness awareness and suicide prevention education. Period.

The Letter and Confirmation

Sixteen months after Wayne's death, his wife, Kathy, hosted a small gathering of some of their closest friends. During the cookout, she started to feel cold and went inside to get a jacket from the closet. One of Wayne's old windbreakers was still there. For some reason she had kept it on her side of their coat closet and grabbed it, though she'd never worn it before. She put it on and continued to enjoy the company. They reminisced about Wayne, and memories of the good times were starting to feel more natural.

Kathy reached into the jacket pocket—maybe for a tissue, maybe to warm her hands, or maybe just out of habit. She felt a piece of paper, pulled it out, unfolded it, and read the words written on it:

Kathy, family & friends,
I love you all.
This depression has gotten the best of me.
Do not blame yourself as it was me.
Please use my illness to help others.
God help me to help others.

Wayne

Our family received some sense of closure from Wayne through that letter. Since Wayne's death, my father had been suffering with silent anger, sometimes saying, "That rascal, why did he do that?"

When I showed him the letter, he said, "I'm proud of Wayne." It was closure for him. My mother said, "Oh, the pain he must have been in. He wrote this letter knowing you were going to find it, Jeff. He knew you would do something about it."

Wayne's request was already being answered months before we found his note. We were well on our way to providing mental illness awareness and suicide prevention education in our community and beyond. However, his letter made me feel like I needed to put things in overdrive. And we did.

Even though it was too late to save Wayne, I could honor the request he left in his last written words. He wanted his experience somehow to help others. Even in his last days, he reached out for us—not to help him, but to help other people going through what he had been going through. This became my mission.

Regardless of all the "ifs" that plagued me—what I might have been able to do for Wayne before he died—there was nothing I could do for him now. But I could honor that request. There were plenty of other people like him who needed help. I had been struggling so much with what else I could have done to help him, but I hadn't known how to recognize the warning signs that were there. And I wouldn't have known what to do even if I had noticed them. But what if we could prevent the same thing from happening to other families? What if there were a tool that could equip people to identify mental illness in others and then help them get the help they need? What if there were a way for people to know what to do? Those are the questions **be nice.** answered for us.

Looking Back—and Looking Ahead

As I mentioned, I have depression. I've taken medication for it since 2011. Major changes in my life triggered my depression, much as life events triggered Wayne's. I didn't consider suicide, although there were times when I would cry during the night wishing I could make the pain end. A cousin died from depression by suicide about thirty years ago, and I remember thinking then that suicide was a very selfish way to die. I had a friend who died by suicide about twelve years ago, and again I had the same feeling. Now I know better. It isn't a selfish act but a simple equation. Those who die by suicide feel that their pain exceeds the gain they think remains in their lives. In their mind, their pain is greater than their gain. Simply put, PAIN > GAIN.

Looking back, I can see how Wayne's pain became greater than his perceived gain. I can now also fit the warning signs into the **be nice.** action plan. I noticed the changes in his behavior after the life-altering event of a bankruptcy that disrupted his lifelong passion, the car business. I noticed his weight loss, his pale complexion, his inability to get out of bed in the morning, his loss of confidence, and so much more. I noticed that he didn't put his boat in the water all summer, that he quit doing a lot of things he loved to do, that he didn't make plans for his usual ski trip that fall, and that he quit enjoying a drink like he used to. He even texted, "I love you." I didn't pick up on that signal but wish I had.

I invited myself to initiate a conversation with Wayne in which I expressed concern about his change in behavior—especially the lack of boating and skiing. I showed love, respect, and concern for him because of these changes I was observing.

But I wish I had known then what I know now about taking the next steps. I accepted Wayne's answers about why he wasn't boating and skiing anymore without challenging him with the tough question: "Are you thinking of killing yourself?"

I empowered him to see a doctor and get on an antidepressant, and I empowered him to go to church and read his Bible. But because I didn't pick up on what he seemed to have been thinking, I couldn't empower myself or him to get more of the professional help he needed.

The **be nice.** action plan provides the knowledge and confidence to take the necessary steps to help a person who is struggling with depression get the help he or she needs. It's a tool that provides the same kind of prevention that "stop, drop, and roll" does for a fire. When we think of someone caught in a fire, we know to give this most basic and urgent advice of stopping, dropping, and rolling.

When we think of someone stuck in depression, we hear silence.

The acrostic **be nice.** is easy to understand and implement in a crisis situation. Not only does it improve lives, it can save lives too. **be nice.** has changed my life and the lives of many others. It is changing the way people think about and respond to mental illness, depression, and potential suicide.

The fact that one out of every four people in the world will suffer with some level of depression or mental illness this year, and that nearly one-half of those people will not seek or receive professional treatment, demands a large-scale response. Depression is a painful but unaddressed illness for those who have it; it's an invisible one for those who don't. That has to change.

That's where we all have an opportunity to help—to arm ourselves with the tools we need to address this illness and help those who are struggling with it. It begins with our loved ones but should extend to friends and acquaintances wherever we're engaged in our communities. That's where you come in. I didn't know how to help Wayne at the time. You have the opportunity to arm yourself with the tools that can help yourself and others.

After reading this book, I am convinced that you will be equipped as I am with the easiest action plan to help change, improve, and save lives from depression and suicide. My hope is that you will help me to carry out my brother Wayne's wishes as well as so many others who have succumbed to mental illness by suicide to help others overcome the illness of depression before it takes more lives.

PART TWO

This depression has gotten has gotten the best of me.

Myths and Understandings

PART TWO

This depression has gotten the best of me.

Myths and Understandings

Headlines announcing a suicide are always jarring and disturbing. They seem to be more common than ever, but we're almost always taken aback by the name, face, and image that go with the story. Each celebrity death is heartbreaking to fans and to our collective consciousness.

Somewhere beneath the shock of that death is a haunting question: If such a beloved person with such apparent success didn't want to live anymore, what went wrong? Are depression and disillusionment really at the end of our ideals for status, popularity, and wealth? Is achieving our dreams and meeting our goals ever really enough? If people who have "made it" discover that making it wasn't worth it, how does that affect our hope for the future?

Think of all the people we have loved via our media who are no longer with us—icons who were still being celebrated but could no longer celebrate their own successes:

- Actors Robin Williams and Margot Kidder

- Fashion designer Kate Spade

- Musicians Curt Cobain, Chris Cornell, Chester Bennington, and Avicii (Tim Bergling)

- Chef Anthony Bourdain

- Authors David Foster Wallace and Hunter Thompson

- Football player Junior Seau

And most of these were just within the last few years. Go back further, and names like Ernest Hemingway, Marilyn Monroe, and numerous other beloved icons comprise a lengthy list.

When a suicide like these is reported, many of us feel a sense of tragic loss. But those feelings are magnified dramatically when suicide hits close to home—when we hear of the death by suicide of a friend, colleague, or family member. We wonder what happened, what must have gone through that person's mind, how their struggles became so unbearable that death seemed preferable. We think of any death as a tragedy, but these more so. They are surrounded not only by the physical pain and trauma of death itself but by a lingering ache of someone not wanting to live anymore. It feels like the most tragic death of all.

Heightening our sense of tragedy is a nagging suspicion that the death could have been prevented. We always ask big "if" questions when we experience a significant loss—if things had been different, if other decisions had been made, if the timing and circumstances had deviated just a little bit this way or that way, we might not be grieving that loss. But those "if" questions get even bigger after a suicide. If someone had noticed the warning signs, if help had been sought earlier, if whatever long-ago decisions shaped the course of this person's life had gone another way, might this tragedy have been prevented?

Suicide prevention is both a desperate need and a real possibility. We simply need to be equipped with the tools to (1) create an accepting, affirming environment in which suicide becomes less and less likely and (2) recognize when someone is severely ill or may be at risk and take steps to intervene. We'll see more specifically how we can be part of the solution in the following chapters, but it begins with understanding. We need to know the nature of this disease if we're going to address it effectively. As we begin to understand its dynamics and its impact, we can prepare ourselves to become the solution we're looking for.

Understanding Mental Illness and Suicide

Written by Christy Buck and Jeff Elhart

Imagine the last time you had a bad case of the flu. You were likely curled up in a ball on a sofa or bed with blankets covering your body from chin to toes. Do you remember what was going through your mind—that feeling of *when is this going to end?* A sense of hopelessness and helplessness? There was nothing you could do except get rest, drink lots of fluids, rest some more, and wait.

You may have felt as if your flu would never end, but you knew it would eventually, probably within a few days. But imagine that sense of hopelessness not for just a few days but for weeks, months, or even years. That's how depression can feel.

Many of the psychological symptoms of the flu mimic the symptoms of psychiatric disorders—a loss of interest in previously enjoyable activities, decreased energy, poor concentration, excessive worry. The way a person feels emotionally when he or she has the flu is the way someone with depression or anxiety tends to feel most of the time. They share psychiatric symptoms.[2]

[2] Steven Schlozman, "Influenza and Your Psyche: The Flu Can Be Pretty Depressing," *Psychology Today*, February 2, 2018, www.psychologytoday.com/us/blog/grand-rounds/201802/influenza-and-your-psyche.

Well-meaning people often try to motivate someone with these symptoms by telling them to "cheer up" or "pull up your bootstraps" or "you'll feel better when you get back to work." Their intentions are good, but their advice doesn't serve the best interests of someone who is struggling with depression or other mental illnesses. There is no easy fix. But there are ways to help. This book offers sensible and accessible tools for recognizing those who are struggling with this silent disease.

There are many mental illnesses, of which depression is only one. Since it is the mental disorder most often linked with suicide, this book will focus primarily on this underlying condition for suicidal thoughts. The action plan we introduce later in the book can be used in a variety of situations but focuses on depression as an occurrence we are most likely to encounter in our interactions with people around us, which will prepare us to help them as effectively as possible.

Understanding Mental Illness

Millions of people are directly affected by mental illness each year. Millions more are affected by association with loved ones struggling with depression, anxiety, or some other mental illness. Virtually everyone is touched.

It's important to understand that, because if mental illness is seen as an uncommon experience, it will continue to be addressed only by specialists and those directly affected. But if we recognize how common it is, it becomes an important issue for all of us. Our whole society needs to understand the psychological, physical, social, and financial impacts of this type of illness. Those struggling need to understand that they are not alone—and certainly not rare oddities. Just knowing the numbers puts us in a position to raise awareness, remove the stigma, and advocate for better care.

Today we have a much better understanding of how the human brain works and how to treat mental illnesses effectively. Neurologists still recognize that there are vast areas of knowledge about mental health that we still lack, but we also have many effective treatments and much more compassion toward those who are suffering than many earlier generations have had. Human beings have tended to marginalize threats and problems they don't understand, but with understanding comes a willingness to embrace the challenge and seek solutions.

People who struggle with depression have been blamed for being "moody" or melancholy and often told to cheer up or get over it. This is an enormous oversimplification and dismissal of the problem. Depression has been misunderstood and unacknowledged as a real issue. It is an illness that can be mild, moderate, or severe. At its most severe, according to the World Health Organization (WHO), it can even be as disabling as quadriplegia.[3]

Depression is often accompanied by a loss of sleep, appetite, interest or enjoyment, energy, sense of self-worth, and/or concentration. These symptoms are generally considered a depressive episode if they last for at least two weeks. Sometimes they recur repeatedly over time (Recurrent Depressive Disorder), and sometimes they alternate with normal moods and manic episodes (Bipolar Affective Disorder). In severely depressive episodes, the sufferer has difficulty continuing with work or other normal activities.

[3] "Depression," World Health Organization, January 30, 2020, www.who.int/news-room/fact-sheets/detail/depression.

Depression is not the result of strictly psychological factors; biology, social interactions, and circumstances can all contribute to the condition. People who have experienced psychological trauma or adverse life events (the death of a loved one, loss of a job, abuse, bankruptcy, health crises, etc.) are more likely to become depressed, but depression can happen to anyone.

Depression is a leading cause of disability worldwide, with more than 264 million affected worldwide.[4] Though many people get discouraged or even what they would call "depressed" from time to time, depression as an illness is not just a mood fluctuation or a temporary response to circumstances. It becomes a serious health condition when it affects decision-making, inhibits normal functioning and work, and adversely affects relationships. Though effective psychological and pharmaceutical treatments are available, many people who struggle with depression are never diagnosed or treated for it. The stigma associated with mental illness is the number one barrier to a person seeking help.

This stigma is one of the reasons that the treatment for depression and many other forms of mental illness begins an average of eleven years after the onset of symptoms. This reluctance is stronger among men than among women. Studies show a general unwillingness among men to acknowledge mental health problems and suicidal thoughts. Even when people know the resources available to them— and very often they don't—they are uncomfortable communicating their deepest feelings to others. In a culture that values self-reliance and independence, asking for help with something as personal as emotional struggles and traumas can be difficult. The pull-up-your-

---

[4] www.who.int/en/news-room/fact-sheets/detail/depression.

bootstraps mentality still runs strong in many cultures. Sometimes the people who need the most help think they shouldn't need any at all.

Still, people are far more willing to talk about their mental health today than they were even three or four decades ago. The stigma is not as strong as in generations past, but that doesn't mean the stigma is gone or that public discourse on this subject is where it needs to be. The stigma and pain of mental disorders and cultural values of independence remain strong in many families and communities.

Leaders in the mental health field are working to reduce barriers like these by increasing awareness, making support more available, and providing effective referrals for treatment. Depression and anxiety are not illnesses people can overcome just by ignoring them and hoping they go away. The more these topics are discussed openly, the more people will be able to reach out when they need help and open up about their own struggles.

Sometimes the willingness is there and the knowledge isn't. Even when people want to reach out, they aren't sure who can help them or where to start. Simply knowing what to do is a huge barrier to overcome in today's mental illness epidemic. Here too, mental health advocates are working tirelessly to increase awareness and provide better-established pathways for people to get the help they need.

How does that translate into your circle of influence and the people you see every day? With some variation for where you live and certain socioeconomic factors, about 20 percent of the adults you run into will experience some form of mental illness in a given year. The number nearly doubles for those who identify as LGBTQI. But less than 45 percent of the U.S. adult population with any kind of mental illness received treatment in 2019. One in six youth (ages 6-17) experience a mental illness each year, but only half of those received any kind of treatment. In other words, many people among our family, friends, coworkers, and other acquaintances are suffering from one kind of mental illness or another, but less than half of them are getting the help they need.[5]

Mental illness has far-reaching ripple effects. People with depression, for example, have a much higher risk of developing cardiovascular and metabolic diseases than others. Rates of unemployment and substance use disorders are far higher among those struggling with mental illness than they are among those who aren't. Families are significantly affected; caregivers of adults with mental or emotional health issues— more than eight million people, in recent studies—spend an average of thirty-two hours a week providing care. Communities are significantly affected too; high percentages of veteran patients, homeless people, and prison populations have a diagnosed mental illness or substance use disorder. And businesses are also profoundly affected, with serious mental illnesses being responsible for nearly $200 billion dollars in lost earnings each year.

Understanding Suicide

Imagine holding your breath as long as you can. By the time you gasp for air, if you're like most adults, another person somewhere in the world will die by suicide—an average of one every forty seconds. Or imagine hitting your snooze button and falling back asleep for ten

---

[5] Statistics in this paragraph are based on reports from SAMHSA and NAMI. www.nami.org/mhstats and www.nami.org/NAMI/media/NAMI-Media/Infographics/NAMI_YouAreNotAlone.

minutes. When you wake up, it's likely another person in the U.S. will have died by suicide.[6]

Those are alarming numbers. According to the Centers for Disease Control and Prevention (CDC), nearly fifty thousand Americans per year (800,000 worldwide) have died by suicide in recent years, which ranks the U.S. somewhere between twenty-five and thirty out of 182 countries for highest suicide rates. Deaths by suicide claim two-and-a-half times the lives of homicides. Suicide ranks tenth among the causes of death in the U.S., but it's the second leading cause of death for people age ten to thirty-four and the fourth leading cause for the thirty-five to forty-five age group. Over the last two decades, suicide rates have increased in every U.S. state other than Nevada, which already had a very high rate. In thirty states, it jumped by 25 percent or more; in some, nearly 50 percent or more. Nationally, it increased 33 percent.

These statistics don't align with what is happening in most other developed countries. According to the World Health Organization (WHO), Great Britain, Canada, China, and the majority of European Union countries have significantly lower rates. In national terms, then, this problem is approaching epidemic proportions.

Suicide is not just a U.S. problem, of course. It occurs throughout the world and affects people of all nations, cultures, religions, and classes. The highest rates are not unique to any particular region; recent statistics showed the top five suicide rates to be scattered among countries on several continents. Though variations occur, statistics generally do not discriminate widely between specific regions and degrees of economic development.

---

[6] Centers for Disease Control and Prevention (CDC).

We know a good bit about national patterns within the U.S. in terms of demographic groups that are most vulnerable to suicide. Recent rates suggest that the highest percentage of suicides occur among men age thirty-five to sixty-four and seventy-five and older. Rates in rural counties are almost twice those in urbanized counties, and because a higher percentage of people in rural states own guns, rural deaths by suicide involve firearms at a greater frequency. In the U.S., the rate for men tends to be roughly four times higher than for women. While black men are ten times more likely to be homicide victims than white men, the latter are two-and-a-half times more likely to die by suicide. Traditionally, suicide rates have been highest among elderly males (with some exceptions globally; in China, for example, women are more likely to kill themselves than men are), but rates among young people have been increasing.

Of course, anyone who has been touched by suicide, whether through the death of a relative, friend, or coworker, knows that numbers don't tell the whole story. They can inform us about the magnitude of the problem, but they can't describe the emotional toll it takes on the people affected. This problem cannot be boiled down to impersonal numbers. It's a deeply personal epidemic with lifelong repercussions for those left behind. Any one of those people can tell us something the numbers can't: addressing this problem simply has to be a priority.

Addressing it can be challenging, though. People who have been affected by a loved one's suicide are often reluctant to talk about their feelings, even though their proximity to a suicide puts them at greater risk. Sometimes the experience is surrounded by shame, as if survivors are somehow part of a problem that reflects poorly on them. The pain of lingering memories is also a hindrance; sometimes conversations about a suicide are just too uncomfortable and reopen wounds that have not fully healed. And the sense that we "ought" to be able to overcome our emotions prevents many from processing their feelings with others.

The Link Between Mental Illness and Suicide

Mental illness and suicide are not the same thing; most people who suffer from a mental illness do not die by suicide. Most people who consider suicide are suffering from some aspect of mental illness. This is where professional treatment begins.

Many health care professionals are trained in suicide prevention, but only in a few states is this kind of training required. It has been widely recommended, but follow-through has been sporadic. Policies vary widely from state to state regarding duration, frequency, and even necessity of training. As a result, not all mental and behavioral health care professionals can recognize someone at risk for suicide and take preventive action. The National Action Alliance for Suicide Prevention, an influential public-private partnership, has advocated for higher and more consistent standards and made suicide prevention a national priority.

But the big difference-maker in reducing suicides is broader knowledge among the general population. Mental health care professionals can't be everywhere, and they don't have their eyes on everyone in our businesses, schools, government offices, places of worship, and homes. Only by bringing education to our communities can we significantly reduce the risk of suicide.

That takes us back to those big questions we ask when we experience a significant loss. How much of this risk can be reduced? And what part can the majority of us who are not mental health professionals do to reduce it? Especially in the aftermath of a suicide, when our hearts are weighed down with grief, we wonder, *If someone had noticed the signs, and if efforts to help had been made earlier, could this tragedy have been prevented?*

The answer to that question in any individual case may be impossible to know. But the answer for suicide in general is a resounding yes. In fact, this book is firmly based on the belief that suicide is not inevitable. The numbers cited above can be decreased, and every one of us can play a part in doing that. The twin convictions that mental illness is treatable and suicide is preventable will come up again and again in these pages. We are not helpless in the face of this growing epidemic.

"Epidemic" may seem like an exaggeration, but that's what the numbers and trends we've looked at are telling us. It may also seem like a specifically medical term for a concern that goes beyond medical causes. But that's where we need to clarify the problem we're up against. Mental illness and suicide *are* medical issues, not just social or psychological ones. They cut across our categories because so many different kinds of factors contribute to them and a multifaceted approach is necessary to combat them. We are sometimes dealing with complex issues that often require the expertise of specialists in a variety of fields.

The good news is that mental illness and suicide don't require *only* the expertise of specialists. The approach of everyday people like us doesn't have to be complex. In fact, it can be quite simple. We can do so much more to create a world and a culture in which these diseases become much less frequent and threatening. That's where solving these problems begins—not at the back end after people have been struggling with mental illness and given in to suicidal thoughts, but at the front end where we relate to people on a day-to-day basis, notice what's going on in their lives, and know how to approach them and help them when we can see that they are struggling. Every one of us is a huge part of the solution to these tragic situations.

Suicide is one of the leading causes of death in the United States and has been on the rise in nearly every state over the last two decades. Ninety percent of people who die by suicide have experienced symptoms of a mental illness,[7] but there are other contributing factors too. People lose hope over broken relationships, lost jobs, financial crises, legal troubles, use and abuse of harmful substances, and significant life changes like the loss of a loved one, homelessness, or a number of other sources of grief, fear, anger, and disappointment. We'll discuss the causes a bit more in the next chapter—and the fact that these experiences are indiscriminate, affecting people from all walks of life—but just knowing how widespread these realities are and how vulnerable human beings can be is step one. We have to learn to see mental health and suicide prevention as priorities.

Making the treatment of mental illness and suicide prevention as

---

[7] National Alliance on Mental Illness (NAMI), "It's Okay to Talk About Suicide," March 2021, www.nami.org/mhstats.

a priority in our society requires an all-hands-on-deck approach. This is not just the domain of special interests. It involves government policies, public health agencies, the health care industry, education initiatives, business plans, media awareness, community organizations, and every member of every family. Some of these entities are better positioned to coordinate efforts, but the effort needs to come from everyone. The mental health of our society requires a comprehensive approach.

As you can gather from the information above—an increasing need and desire for suicide prevention combined with cultural, social, and knowledge barriers that inhibit intervention—we need more resources to be able to do this. Many of the resources currently available are wonderful and effective, but considering the size of the problem, we don't have enough to sufficiently increase awareness, advocate for action, educate and equip people to identify people who are struggling and know what to do in response, and empower people to seek treatment. And we don't currently have well-trained eyes everywhere that can spot the needs in people's lives and address them appropriately. That's why we all need well-trained eyes. This book is one effort to fill the gap, and the information and action plan in the following pages can go a long way toward preparing readers to help make a significant, lifechanging difference.

chapter

4

Nobody Is Immune

Written by Christy Buck and Jeff Elhart

Marie was overwhelmed at work, frustrated at home, and feeling more helpless and hopeless by the day. It wasn't difficult to see why. The hormonal changes from her pregnancy, the pressure of making major decisions as a corporate leader, and circumstances like her husband's unemployment and an antagonistic colleague would have made a lot of people anxious and irritable.

But Marie's anxious and irritable moods were more than mild, temporary symptoms. They were affecting her family life and her career. She was missing appointments and losing her concentration. Her co-workers could tell something was wrong. She wasn't her usual self.

At her next doctor's appointment, Marie told her obstetrician that she was having trouble sleeping and maintaining her focus. "I can't concentrate at work as I used to."

Her doctor asked a few questions—how long these symptoms had been occurring, if they were present in her previous pregnancies, and if anyone in her family had ever been diagnosed with depression. Marie wasn't sure how relevant the questions were, but her doctor explained that she was experiencing signs of depression. She referred Marie to another specialist who could offer treatment for mental health.

Marie realized later that the evidence was right in front of her. She had noticed the changes but had not related them to mental health. She had seen her father struggle with depression and thought she understood the disease but didn't realize her symptoms were related to depression until her doctor explained that she was at risk and set her on the path to a healthier life. Marie began exercising regularly and taking time with her family to have fun. Her home life and work life began to improve dramatically.

Marie's depression was noticed by a physician, but many people struggle with the disease out of sight from a medical professional. Denard, for example, was a high school student who suffered a serious knee injury in a basketball game. During his recovery, he lost his motivation, withdrew from friends, lost interest in school and sports, felt constantly fatigued, and became prone to outbursts of anger. He felt hopeless and didn't understand why.

Denard's parents were supportive, but they didn't have the tools to recognize what was going on in his mind—the guilt, self-criticism, and self-blame; his impaired concentration and loss of appetite; his lack of energy and over-sleeping. His dad kept pushing him to get back on the court again. His mom just wanted him to get well.

Fortunately, Denard's coach had been through something similar and recognized the signs. After breaking up a fight between Denard and a teammate, the coach sat down with him for a talk.

"What's going on with you lately? Your parents reached out to me. They're concerned. Your attitude has been poor, your grades are slipping, you're not eating."

"You just don't get it," Denard said.

"I was once in your shoes," the coach explained. "Best player on the team. Recruiters were after me. Then the summer after my senior year, in summer training, I cut left and tore my ACL. I lost my scholarship and just about everything else. My family stepped in and got me into therapy."

Denard shook his head. "I don't think my parents would ever go for that."

"What if we talked to them together?" the coach offered.

Denard agreed and ended up getting the help he needed—with a little persistence and overcoming his father's skepticism. Denard now realizes that his physical injury wasn't the problem; it was a risk factor that made depression more likely. After a few therapy sessions, his symptoms began to fade, his appetite returned to normal, he stopped isolating himself, and he felt empowered to embrace the people around him. He started to feel like himself again.

Maddie, another student at Denard's school, was struggling for different reasons. She was stressed about a major college entrance exam, and she was obsessive about studying for it. Part of her obsession was due to a desire for perfection; another part was her desire to avoid home. Her mother drank a lot and often wasn't available when Maddie needed her.

But Maddie would have to depend on her mother to get her to the test. Buses weren't running that morning, and Maddie needed a ride. She told her mother in advance, reminded her repeatedly when her mother arrived home the night before—heavily intoxicated—and tried to get her mother out of bed the next morning to drive her.

"You can drive," her mom mumbled. "Keys are on the table."

Maddie couldn't drive. She grabbed her bicycle, pedaled as fast as she could to the school, and arrived after the main entrance was locked and a "Testing in Progress" sign was posted on the classroom door.

Maddie felt like she couldn't breathe. She began crying, pacing in the hallway, and panicking over the missed test. She sat down, through the tears saw a **be nice.** flyer with a number on it for those who "need help," and tried to explain what was going on to the voice on the other end.

The person answering the number—the National Suicide Prevention Lifeline—talked her through the crisis. "I need you to breathe, okay? . . . I'm putting you through to someone who can help. It's going to be okay."

Maddie doesn't remember how long she spent on the phone, but within minutes of talking to someone, she realized that the panic attack she had been experiencing was not really about the test or about her mother. It was about years of anxiety, shame, and trying to keep it all inside. She scheduled a local appointment for that afternoon and took a major step toward a healthier life.

These three examples of people struggling with mental health concerns are diverse in categories of age, ethnicity, and backgrounds, yet they all had a few things in common: deep and intense struggles, problems, or feelings that seemed bigger than they could handle, and an unawareness of how they could get the kind of help that could save their lives.

Mental illness does not discriminate. Depression is on the rise, affecting young people at an alarming rate while taking its greatest numbers from people in their middle-age years and later. In ongoing, untreated cases, depression and anxiety can lead to suicidal thoughts, ultimately stealing a productive present and future from individuals, families, communities, and society as a whole.

Why Do People Die by Suicide?

Imagine feeling like you are stuck in a deep, dark hole—as if you're in some altered state of existence in which life is going on all around you but you are somehow unable to participate in it. Maybe it feels like you're drowning in a vast ocean, constantly treading water even though you've already exhausted all your energy, desperate for any kind of escape. At times, you might feel like a ghost of a person walking around in an exterior shell, and no one really sees or cares. Sometimes you think your own brain has turned against you, and there's nothing you can do to stop it. All you can do is look for some way of escape. Whatever dreams, passions, goals, and plans you once had are a distant, empty memory. You just want to end the pain, the fear, and the shame.

These are common descriptions of experiences with suicide ideation.[8] These descriptions vary from person to person—it can be very difficult to put words around these feelings—but many of the same

---

[8] For more descriptions of suicidal thinking from those who have experienced it, see https://themighty.com/2016/12/what-being-suicidal-feels-like.

themes and images appear again and again. Most people struggling with these thoughts feel overwhelmed, if they feel much at all. Some describe numbness, hopelessness, even a sense of being dead already. Some feel like a stranger in their own skin, hardly recognizing the person they see in the mirror. Most wonder if they will be missed—if there is anyone who would help them if they asked, as if they are an unbearable burden to the people around them, if they are noticed at all. For those who feel as if they are screaming inside, it's a silent scream that no one else can hear.

Suicide ideation is usually accompanied by one or more of a variety of discernible risk factors. Risk factors are not necessarily causes of suicide, but they are situations or conditions that can increase the possibility of suicide. The CDC lists the following risk factors as examples:[9]

Individual

- Previous suicide attempt

- Mental illness, such as depression

- Social isolation

- Criminal problems

- Financial problems

- Impulsive or aggressive tendencies

- Job problems or loss

- Legal problems

- Serious illness

---

[9] "Risk and Protective Factors," Centers for Disease Control and Prevention (CDC), January 25, 2021, www.cdc.gov/suicide/factors.

- Substance use disorder

Relational

- Adverse childhood experiences such as child abuse and neglect
- Bullying
- Family history of suicide
- Relationship problems such as a break-up, violence, or loss
- Sexual violence and abuse

Community

- Barriers to health care
- Cultural and religious beliefs, such as a belief that suicide is a noble resolution of a personal problem
- Suicide cluster in the community

Societal

- Stigma associated with mental illness or help-seeking
- Easy access to lethal means such as firearms or medications
- Unsafe media portrayals of suicide

The connection between these risk factors and the possibility of suicide is clear in some cases, but some warrant further explanation:

- **Medications**: Some drugs (e.g., corticosteroids, isotretinoin [for acne], interferon-alpha [antiviral], and others) can increase a person's risk of depression.

- **Conflict:** Personal disputes or friction with family members or friends usually aren't enough to trigger depression by themselves but can contribute to depression in someone who is already vulnerable to it.

- **Genetics:** A family history of depression may increase the risk. It's a complex trait—generally many different genes exert small effects rather a single gene causing it.

- **Major events:** Everyone experiences stressful life events (e.g., losing a job, getting divorced) or even positive experiences like retirement or moving to a new home. But not everyone experiences depression from these stresses. Clinical depression goes beyond normal responses to these stressful events.

- **Abuse:** Physical, sexual, or emotional abuse can increase a person's vulnerability to clinical depression later in life.

- **Substance abuse:** A significant percentage of people with substance abuse problems also have major or clinical depression. This can create a vicious cycle; using substances like alcohol and drugs can make depression worse, yet people tend to turn toward them when they feel down.

The exact causes of depression, the leading cause of suicide, are hard to identify, but many of these contributing factors are not. Depression usually results from a combination of issues that include recent events and long-term physical and mental patterns. It can have both physiological and socio-psychological elements—or, to put it another way, aspects of both "nature" and "nurture." Its causes are a mixture of brain chemistry, genetics, habitual thoughts, circumstances, and much more.

Most of these risk factors represent continuing conditions or difficulties, which are more likely to cause depression than recent life stressors. But if a person has already experienced depression, a recent experience like a job loss or relational breakup can trigger it again. The list of risk factors above is not exhaustive, but it does suggest that most or all of us have been affected by one or more of them or know someone who is currently experiencing them.

If you have experience with depression yourself, you know what its symptoms feel like. If not, you may be curious—and wonder why a depressed person can't just "snap out of it." If that's true of you, think back to that illustration we opened with in chapter 3. Imagine feeling flu-like fatigue for weeks, months, or even years, with no energy to get up and do anything about it. Getting started each day can feel like pushing a boulder up a hill, only to have it roll back down before the start of the next day. Things that should take a few minutes to do can sometimes take hours. Heaviness, lethargy, indecision, and indifference can be constant conditions. Sometimes depressed people have been dealing with these feelings and symptoms for so long that they begin to accept them as normal.

Clearly this is a serious issue. People who are depressed say they are unhappy with life in general, and the causes can include innate disorders of the mind and sequences of events that prompt feelings of despair, dread, loneliness, and hopelessness. Depression can be short-term or long-term, physiological and/or psychological, related to circumstances and/or related to deeply ingrained mental habits.

It is an extremely complex issue with multiple underlying factors, any of which can trigger suicidal thoughts. Addressing all the root causes would require professional expertise. Fortunately, that is available for those who seek it. And, also fortunately, the rest of us can notice symptoms and address them without having to understand all the causes and contributing factors.

Suicide Knows No Categories

Depression and suicide do not discriminate between ages, but they do affect different age groups in different ways. For example:

- **Retirement age and above.** It is not unusual for people to know what they are retiring from without knowing exactly what they are retiring to. Retirement years can be filled with new adventures and activities, but many people lose their sense of purpose after retirement and may begin to wonder what remains for them to live for. In addition, people with other diseases like cancer, cardiovascular disease, and diabetes—by no means exclusive to older populations but certainly more common among them—are more vulnerable to depression, and depression makes people more vulnerable to these diseases.

- **Midlife.** Most Americans who die from suicide are working-class, middle-aged men. The reasons for this include the well-known phenomenon of "midlife crisis," but a number of other factors contribute to depression and suicide in this age group, and not just for men or the working class. The economic uncertainties of approaching retirement and the sense that savings may never be "enough"; a recession, which exacerbates personal economic insecurity; job loss, which creates the same financial worries and is becoming more common in an era in which few people work at one company their whole lives; the empty-nest syndrome, which leaves many couples wondering what life together looks like if it is no longer fully preoccupied with and centered on raising the children; and divorce, which can leave many in this age group with an unsettling feeling of "starting over" and wondering if it's too late to find fulfillment in a relationship.

- **Younger generations.** Our period in history presents some challenges for teenagers and young adults. Culture is changing rapidly. Stresses are coming earlier. Past generations could usually rely on steady jobs in stable companies, but with the constantly shifting business landscape today, uncertainties abound. There are fewer clear paths to success, and even those people with a well-planned future are often preparing for or coming into the workforce with lots of education debt and little security in the positions they seek. And they are navigating all of these uncertainties with less in-person social contact to lean on.

Technology creates many new opportunities, but it also increases the field of competition in areas as diverse as job-seeking and dating. Teenagers and young adults see all the options out there, but they also see all the competition for them. It's right in front of their faces, and it's constant. If someone is comparing his or her life to all the ideal images that are being presented online—usually inaccurately—the comparisons inevitably fall short. (For example, everyone online knows his or her own worst secrets and embarrassing faults but, buffered by virtual distancing, rarely sees the flaws of others in their social network. One's real self versus everyone else's ideal self is always an unfair comparison.) It's easy in that virtual environment to feel squeezed out, marginalized, and vulnerable. The fear of missing out—in relationships, job opportunities, and many other experiences—is dramatically intensified by the ever-present flood of unattainable possibilities.

Many studies suggest that the increase of screen time on smartphones and social media correlates with increased mental health issues. It's hard to isolate factors and determine direct cause-and-effect influences—many other variables parallel these increases too—but the trends at least represent some serious warning signals. Young people who spend a lot of time online may become more depressed for a variety of reasons—changes in thinking patterns, loss of sleep, loss of direct personal relationships, and an almost complete loss of privacy—but regardless of the reason, the numbers are unsettling. It's possible that much of the increase in cases of mental illness is due to increased *reports* of these cases—that a percentage of current numbers had been there all along but went unreported because the stigma and shame of seeking help was stronger in the past than it is now—but that's not the only explanation. Our youth are struggling with trends, technological issues, and social environments that are un-precedented in history.

These problems are not unique to young people. Social media can be inherently divisive regardless of a person's age. Every comment is subject to incivility, every image can serve as a form of self-marketing, and the best and worst of people's lives often play out in public, pushing us toward superficiality and shaming those who have the misfortune of having their embarrassing moments recorded and posted for all to see. But these dynamics are magnified in a generation that does not remember a time before smartphones, and the mental health impact is greater as they learn to live in this environment.

That's really the message of this chapter. No age group is immune to suicide caused by depression, other mental illness, or adverse circumstances. The point of these statistics and explanations of causes is not to give any demographic group less reason to worry than another. It's to demonstrate that suicide, a preventable tragedy, is not an uncommon crisis that affects only a few. Every death by suicide impacts hundreds, sometimes even thousands, of people, and those people come from every part of our community.

The response to this crisis, therefore, needs to come from every part of our communities. This is not only "their" problem; it should be "our" problem. Together, we can dramatically reduce the occurrences of tragedies like these wherever they happen to be found.

For immediate assistance with suicidal thoughts, call the National Suicide Prevention Lifeline at 1-800-273-TALK.

chapter
5

Dispelling the Myths

Written by Christy Buck and Jeff Elhart

People who see depression and suicide from afar often buy into false stereotypes. While many stereotypes in any area of life are based on real experiences, they also tend to distort them. Stereotypes are over-simplifications, and they miss the many details, complexities, layers, and exceptions that are necessary to understand if we are going to approach the problem with any effectiveness. They depersonalize a very personal issue. We need to give a fuller picture of people who attempt to take their lives.

This chapter dispels myths and answers questions. Why do people die by suicide? Did they die because of a weakness? Are they looking for attention and sympathy? Is suicide hereditary or genetic? Can it be inspired by the suicides of family or friends? Are suicide attempts "cries for help"? Once a person decides to take his or her life, can that person be stopped, or is suicide inevitable?

All of these questions come from the uncomfortable yet under-standable gap between a genuine desire to understand this trag-edy and a reluctance to talk about it in depth. After all, suicide is not a pleasant conversation piece. If we're going to fill that gap, we will need to address the stereotypes and assumptions people make about victims of suicide.

The Facts About Suicide

Most people don't think about suicide until it intersects with their life—usually in the aftermath of the tragic death of a loved one, friend, co-worker, fellow student, or community member. That's when questions come to the surface, and sometimes it can be hard separating what's true from what isn't. Misunderstandings about the reasons someone took his or her life abound.

There is no simple answer to the question of why people take their own life.[10] In cases of mental illness, the issue is a brain that is not functioning as it should. Like any other organ of the body, brains can get sick, and the result is thoughts, feelings, and behaviors that create distortions in the way people perceive themselves and the outside world. Mental illness clearly doesn't always lead to suicide. Many people live with these conditions for much of their lives, and the vast majority of people who struggle with depression never attempt suicide. But when these conditions linger, suicide has to be considered a risk.

A suicide attempt is not a cry for sympathy but can be a cry for help. It's a huge warning sign that was usually preceded by many other subtler warning signs. It can be an expression of hopelessness or unbearable emotional pain—an attempt to get the pain to end or to escape despair. Most people who attempt suicide don't actually

---

[10] Much of the information in this section on facts and myths of suicide is adapted from and indebted to material found at www.save.org.

want to die; in fact, many are later very relieved that their attempt did not end in their death. They were looking for an end to their pain and suffering, but if they had known there were effective ways to deal with their suffering, they may have chosen to pursue them.

Not only is a suicide attempt *not* a matter of getting sympathy or attention; the victim is often not focused on how other people will feel if they died or believes other people would be better off without them. It is a cry for help that needs to be taken seriously. Someone who has attempted suicide is at greater risk of a future attempt without intervention and treatment.

Depression and related mental illnesses have physical and genetic components; a suicide death can put family members and other loved ones at risk. Even though people who have been exposed to the suicide of a friend or acquaintance do not generally have an increased risk of suicide themselves, that exposure can increase the likelihood for those who also carry other risk factors, like depression.

Sometimes people with suicidal thoughts seem to feel better once they have made the decision to kill themselves. This could be because they have given up the fight, see the end of their pain, and feel a sense of release. It can also signal a period of increased energy. If a depressed person's energy returns and hopelessness remains, they may find the ability to act on their suicidal thoughts.

Those who are depressed often experience either an intense emotion like desperation, anxiety, or rage, but sometimes experience a lack of emotions, like indifference or hopelessness. Many people have the idea that if a person feels that much pain, they ought to have enough energy and awareness to seek help. A lot of factors can lead to someone not seeking help; lack of energy, lack of awareness, stigma, and lack of resources available are all part of the problem. Mental illness in general, and depression specifically, can make a person feel helpless and hopeless. Getting help seems futile. And confronting common perceptions surrounding mental illness can often create an insurmountable barrier to reaching out.

When talking about suicide, we need to use proper language in order to dispel myths. Talking about someone who "committed suicide" is common, but the phrase can come across with hints of judgment in it.[11] Adjectives like "successful" suicide, "unsuccessful" suicide, and "failed attempt" inappropriately define a suicide death as a success and a nonfatal attempt as a failure. Terms such as "committed" suicide (associated with crimes) can reinforce stigmatizing attitudes about people who die by suicide. Use terms like "died by suicide," "completed suicide," and "attempted suicide," instead of "successful suicide," "unsuccessful suicide," "failed attempt," or "committed suicide."[12] It's better to say someone "died by suicide" or even was "a victim of suicide," which in the first case reflects objectivity, and in the second acknowledges the tragedy of being harmed by one's own illness (much in the same way we talk about a victim of cancer).

Around three-quarters of the people who die by suicide are male, but about three-quarters of those who attempt suicide are female. The reason for this discrepancy may be the different means of taking one's own life. Men tend to use firearms and other lethal methods

---

[11] Information in this and the following paragraphs is adapted from and indebted to the American Foundation for Suicide Prevention (AFSP).

[12] "Tips for Messaging Safely," National Action Alliance for Suicide Prevention, accessed April 21, 2021, https://suicidepreventionmessaging.org/safety/tips-messaging-safely.

more frequently; women tend to use medications, which allow time for rescue or sometimes aren't as lethal as thought. Younger people, who generally have less access to guns and medications, tend to take their lives more often in other ways. People who are habitual users of alcohol or drugs tend to be more impulsive and are at a higher risk for suicide, by any means, than others.

Many people believe that suicides are more frequent around holidays, especially at the end of the year, when families often gather and lost loved ones are most noticeably missing. There are clear reasons for this assumption. People who are isolated from other family members or whose family situations are more disheartening may feel loneliest during this time of year. And these occasions often bring back many memories, and for those who have experienced significant losses like death or divorce, those memories can be especially painful. But December is actually not when suicides are most frequent; in fact, just the opposite. Suicide rates are higher in the spring and at their lowest in the winter.

The reasons suicides are more common in spring are not fully under-stood. The springtime peak may be the result of a loss of hope as the weather warms but life doesn't seem to improve for the depressed per-son. Or increased sociality during warmer months could put extra pres-sure on someone who is struggling. Some scientists even believe that inflammation from spring allergens could exacerbate mental illness.[13]

Suicide of a family member puts that family at risk, just as mental illnesses like depression do genetically, and we need to treat these risks just as we do risks of family history of physical illnesses like heart

---

[13] International Archives of Allergy and Immunology.

disease, cancer, or diabetes. People with suicide or mental illness in their family history should be especially careful to look for signs and symptoms in themselves, seeking a professional assessment long before those symptoms become unmanageable, but an occurrence of suicide in the family does not automatically mean other members in the family are likely to die by suicide too. Statistically the risk is higher, but the knowledge of the devastating effects of suicide on families is greater too. No one deeply affected by another person's suicide should assume that they are likely to head in that direction too.

Suicides are often portrayed in movies and popular imagination as the result of a catastrophic life event or an extraordinarily stressful situation—a devastating betrayal, an impending arrest, a broken relationship, or a life-threatening diagnosis. Suicide can occur in situations like these, but it hardly ever does without other factors contributing too. Painful experiences can prompt emotions like sadness, despair, anger, or anxiety—sometimes even a fleeting thought that death would be preferable to the pain—but these are usually temporary. Suicidal thoughts are not natural responses to life events. They are almost always the product of a mental illness. If such events trigger suicidal thoughts or actual plans to take one's own life, depression or another mental illness is probably present.

We've seen that depression is a complex disease that can be caused by a variety (and usually a mixture) of factors. Observable changes take place in the brain of someone who becomes depressed, but the chemistry behind those changes can be either genetically inherited or prompted by new thought and behavior patterns (or both). Some people seem to become depressed for no apparent reason, others in the aftermath of painful circumstances or major life changes. Substances, whether alcohol or medications, can also cause or intensify depression.

People who die by suicide don't always appear to be depressed. Depression is usually observable in someone's changing behavior or moods, but sometimes a person could be used to hiding how they are thinking, acting, and feeling. They might seem to be coping well. The moods we would typically expect to see in a depressed person—sadness, crying, lethargy, lack of enthusiasm—are not always visible. Sometimes they are expressed in other ways, as through anger or bitterness or irritability. And sometimes people who take their own lives are genuinely not depressed. Suicide is sometimes a response to extreme anxiety or a different illness like substance use disorder.

Asking someone about suicide is highly unlikely to plant the idea in his or her mind and increase the risk, contrary to some people's worries. People with suicidal thoughts have already come to them independently of suggestions. Telling someone you are concerned for them and want to know if they are thinking about killing themselves is far more likely to provide them with hope for recovery because they know someone cares. Direct questions shared in a compassionate way can encourage someone to open up. If the person seems to be reluctant to answer, it may be that he or she has a plan and does not want to be stopped. If the person's response reveals that he or she has a plan in place, it's time to take immediate action and get help.

Shouldn't Suicide Rates Be Declining?

The fact that rates of mental illness and suicide have risen in several of the last few years seems counterintuitive to many people. We have more options and opportunities in front of us today than ever before. We have better technology for making life easier and overcoming challenges than ever before. On average, people are making more money than ever before. We are connected to greater numbers of people than ever before. On the surface, all of these factors would seem to suggest that life is getting easier and less stressful.

It isn't hard to see why this isn't the case when we really think about it. A greater number of options and opportunities—for careers, relationships, hobbies, travel, and so much more—can actually lead to increased stress. Making a decision can seem overwhelming, even paralyzing, and the fear of making the wrong decision can be terrifying and exhausting. (This is one of the problems of "overchoice," a term coined by Alvin Toffler in Future Shock.) And since we can't choose everything available to us, we already know we are missing out, even before a choice is made. Some level of disappointment seems to be built into the decision-making process. Compared to past generations, we have an unprecedented number of stresses to face when deciding what to do, how and when to do it, where to go, who to be with, and so on.

The problem with having better technology than ever before is that it hasn't reduced our workload. If anything, it has increased our workload and made it more present. Many people who used to leave their work behind at the end of the day now have constant reminders of it and extra hours to put in on it through twenty-four-hour connectedness on multiple devices. The ability to do things more quickly with time-saving devices historically hasn't given us more time in the day. It has raised expectations for productivity. We are as busy—or busier—

than we have ever been, and therefore experiencing higher levels of stress on a daily basis than most previous generations have.

Financial success has simply proven the old adage that money can't buy happiness. In fact, it very often reveals an underlying emptiness; those who thought they would be fulfilled when they had enough find either (1) that there's never enough or (2) that "enough" just doesn't satisfy. And if having enough doesn't satisfy, what does? People climbing the ladder of success can look back over their lives and realize they were on the wrong ladder the whole time. Our relatively affluent lifestyles can raise serious questions about the meaning of life and create something of an existential crisis.[14]

Even though we are connected to greater numbers of people than ever before—we literally see hundreds and thousands of "friends" identified on many social media profiles—we are not connected *deeply* to greater numbers of people. In fact, many would argue that our connections have become more comparative and competitive and less compassionate. Our relational networks have broadened enormously but shallowed out significantly. As a result, many people know hundreds of other people but have very few heart-to-heart connections. This creates a fascinating but sad phenomenon: multitudes of people who are extremely lonely in spite of being surrounded by multitudes of other people who are extremely lonely.

Jim Folk at AnxietyCentre.com lists many of these and other reasons for depression, anxiety, and mental health disorders in general rising among younger generations:[15]

---

[14] Most people would not call themselves affluent, but nearly everyone living in developed countries has access to far more financial resources than the vast majority of people throughout history

[15] Jim Folk, medically reviewed by Marilyn Folk, BScN, with www.AnxietyCentre.com.

- Increased parental pressures

- Increased adoption of electronic media (Electronic Screen Syndrome)

- Increased performance pressures (education, career, financial, etc.)

- Increased terrorist events and threats

- Increase in divisive news

- Dramatic increase in violent TV programs, movies, and video games

- Dramatic increase in graphic children's media

- Increase in sexually explicit material (TV programs, movies, video games, online, etc.)

- Social media pressure

- Reduced face-to-face interactions and social supports

- The breakdown of the family unit

- Sexual orientation questioning

- Gender dysphoria

- Being exposed to a multitude of opinions (on TV and online)

- Being exposed to aggressive behavior (a dramatic rise in child abuse, adult abuse, sexual abuse, etc.)

- Poor/reduced sleep

- Reduced parental contact—children are prematurely separating from parents and families, and bonding to peers

- Increased financial pressure on parents

- Easy access to, and the acceptance of, recreational drugs (of all types)

- Overly protected/indulged children

- Reduced expectations for young adults

- The "I" generation (where everyone believes they are entitled to whatever they want, from opinions to lifestyle choices, and whenever and however they want it)

Not all of these are easily or quickly addressed, but families can take the lead in creating the kind of environment that reduces the risk of depression and anxiety in children and teenagers. Changing the culture at large is an overwhelming task. Being aware of these challenges our young people face and setting them up for emotional health is something we can begin to address today.

These and other social trends have made maintaining mental health much more of a challenge than it once was. The good news is that we have much better resources and treatments than in other eras of history. The bad news is that the escalation of incidences of mental illness—actual and reported—seems to be outpacing the expansion of resources for dealing with them. Social changes are affecting everyone, especially younger generations.

Just as we need many (if not most) of the people in our communities to be trained in CPR, we all need to help mental health professionals by having a basic tool to get someone to appropriate professional help during or before a mental health crisis. Equipping the general population to be mutual "lifeguards" or "first responders"—for everyone to be able to notice symptoms of mental illness and suicidal ideation—would go a long way toward alleviating the problem. Even before that, cultivating a culture of mutual respect, honor, dignity, and friendliness could ward off many mental health issues before they even take root. We need to change the emotional climate of our families, workplaces, schools, and communities for the better, and we need people who notice and reach out when someone is not getting the full benefit of that positive environment and is wrestling with deep emotional challenges. In other words, we need to work together to reduce depression and anxiety on the front end and to recognize and identify it on the back end—*and* to know what to do about it when necessary.

Please use my illness to help others.

The **be nice.** *Action Plan*

PART THREE

Please use my illness to help others.

The **be nice.** Action Plan

You're about to meet a simple tool to potentially change and save a life. You will see how this tool has an impact on the way people think, act, and feel. It gets to the heart and explains what to do to help someone before they reach a point of crisis. Jeff Elhart dubbed it the "stop, drop, and roll" of mental health and suicide prevention.

The "nice" in **be nice.** is an acronym for notice, invite, challenge, and empower. Those steps won't always be administered in that order. In fact, by providing the positive nature of noticing what is good and right about people and creating that culture, we may not need to invite, challenge, or empower. But we can if necessary. The fact that 20 percent of people have depression or a mental health disorder calls for us to be equipped with a logical and simple action plan like **be nice.** to help change and improve lives, and even save them. The next five chapters will provide you with the steps to take action when you or someone you know is experiencing a mental health concern or crisis.

Notice what is right so you can notice what is different. Invite yourself to reach out and have a caring conversation with that person. Challenge stigma by exploring why he or she is exhibiting these changes, and challenge yourself to ask an important, direct question in a mental health crisis. Lastly, empower with resources and knowledge of next steps to get help. Go a step further and empower yourself to stay by their side and assist when appropriate. That may mean connecting them with professional help—a counselor, psychologist, emergency room, or primary care physician. It might include a call to the twenty-four-hour national suicide hotline at 1-800-273-8255 or a text of "go" to 741741.

Has this worked? Are all these efforts making a difference?

Experts from Grand Valley State University conducted an evidence-based study of the use of **be nice.** in schools and found that it has been very effective in increasing mental health awareness and a student's likelihood to seek help for a mental health concern, decreasing the number of behavioral referrals throughout the year. Through qualitative on-site observations and interviews at elementary, middle, and high schools, the study found the **be nice.** program to be effective in creating a positive school climate. Through quantitative analysis of pre– and post–**be nice.** data, the study found a significant reduction in negative schoolwide behaviors. Aspects of this study are still ongoing, but the early phases have shown remarkable effectiveness in decreasing incidences of bullying and behavioral referrals. The study attributes much of the success to the program's creation of a common and unique language for mental illness and suicide prevention.

be nice. is not difficult to learn or implement, but it will require a proactive approach and an intention to follow through, and it's worth it. You may very well change, improve, or save a life.

A Program and an Action Plan

Written by Christy Buck

be nice. was created in 2010 after the suicide of a student at Rutgers University made national headlines and locally sparked a high demand for information and action from the Mental Health Foundation of West Michigan. The MHF had been educating students and the community surrounding mental health since 2005, and Tyler Clementi's tragic death challenged me and my team to expand our programming.

Questions started pouring in. "What are you doing about cyberbullying and bullycide?" "How are you helping kids who are struggling?" With all the awareness raised by this high-profile event, the MHF was called to action. While plenty was going on in terms of training sessions and public services, more needed to be done, and it needed to be more comprehensive than bullying awareness education—a key issue related to mental health, but only one of many.

I called my coworker with a simple idea. "Let's use the words '**be nice**' with a period at the end in all lowercase. I'll be at the office in twenty minutes." Upon my arrival, my coworker, Larissa Payton, had the glowing green logo up on the screen. With the suggestion of a board member, the period was changed to the color pink for emphasis.

First, T-shirts were made with a **be nice.** logo on them, hoping to remind people of the importance of things like respect, kindness, civility, and dignity—that the way we treat each other has an effect on our mental health. I put my kids in the T-shirts and next thing we knew, everyone from classmates, teachers, and parents wanted one of their own. We had success getting the T-shirts into many of the schools where we were doing mental health education, and they started selling by the thousands.

Then we received a call from a school asking if the **be nice.** initiative had an assembly to go with the shirt. An assembly? Sure! Our small and mighty team made up of AmeriCorps members, contract social workers, and administrative staff, some of whom are still on the team today, put together an assembly with some activities to build awareness, and it worked. The MHF was invited to do the same assembly in another school in that district, and that went well too. The team realized there had to be more to it than simply building awareness to deal with the problem. We needed substance, a plan, something to equip people to take action.

That's when the **be nice.** action plan was born. The team prepared for the next assembly by creating the action plan you will read about in the next four chapters—notice, invite, challenge, and empower. We wanted to address more than bullycide. Again, the MHF hoped we could help people understand that the way human beings treat each other has a profound effect on our mental health. We pride ourselves as being the only organization in the area that was connecting the dots between bullying and its relation to mental health and suicide. The staff was empowered to equip as many people with this tool as possible.

be nice. is a program that utilizes an action plan to implement change at both the macro and micro levels. At the macro level, **be nice.** cultivates psychologically safe communities—schools, businesses, faith institutions, and organizations—that foster connectedness and make it okay to talk about mental health, illness, and suicide.

be. The "be" in **be nice.** is a reminder to "be aware." This is a lifestyle.

nice. The "nice" in **be nice.** is an acronym that provides the action plan.

- **notice** what is right and different.

- **invite** yourself to reach out.

- **challenge** stigma.

- **empower** yourself and others with education and resources.

Period. You'll notice that whenever **be nice.** is written in this text, it ends with a period—even in the middle of a sentence (like this one). That's because the action plan means, "That's it. Nothing more, nothing less. It's that simple."

The ultimate goal is for every individual in our communities to have the knowledge to take action when it comes to mental health. This is what we call an upstream approach. We like to use the following narrative to explain what it means to be upstream:

Imagine a large river with a high waterfall. At the bottom of this waterfall hundreds of people are working frantically trying to save those who have fallen into the river and have fallen down the waterfall, many of them drowning. As the people along the shore are trying to rescue as many as possible, one individual looks up and sees a seemingly never-ending stream of people falling down the waterfall and begins to run upstream. One of the other rescuers hollers, "Where are you going? There are so many people that need help here." To which the man replied, "I'm going upstream to find out why so many people are falling into the river."[16]

So how do we bring mental illness awareness and suicide prevention upstream? It's simple: **be nice**. Several major factors increase the likelihood of suicidal ideation (the thought of taking one's own life): things like mental illness, sexual abuse, domestic violence, and substance abuse. Until we understand that these trauma-induced or psychological illnesses are negatively affecting people's quality of life, we will not be able to wrap our arms around the epidemic of suicide.

That has been our goal from the beginning, even before the **be nice**. action plan. The action plan itself is very effective and indispensable for those times when someone may be at risk or has even expressed suicidal thoughts or behaviors. Many people are equipped with the lifesaving tools of CPR for a physical crisis; similarly, we need to be equipped with the proper tools to handle a mental health crisis.

As the team at the MHF worked tirelessly to change the way students learned and addressed mental health concerns within their

---

[16] This illustration is adapted from a story told by Irving Zola and used in an article by John B. McKinlay, "A Case for Refocusing Upstream: The Political Economy of Illness," originally published by the American Heart Association (AHA) in 1975.

communities, several people entered into the picture to help shape the program into what it is today, one of whom was Jeff. The program had been making its way into schools and communities for five years when Jeff made the phone call to the MHF to request its presence as a resource table at an event. That phone call turned into the beginning of a new friendship that would help continue the expansion of the **be nice.** program across the Michigan lakeshore.

During that initial visit, these were the questions on Jeff's mind as he was processing Wayne's death:

- Why are so many people suffering from depression, and why are some of them dying by suicide?

- How do you feel about that?

- What are you going to do about it?

Some people try to come up with the "right" answers; others shut themselves down from trying to come up with any answers at all. But if you allow yourself to be vulnerable to face life's tough battles, you equip yourself to overcome life's hurdles. And in the process, your experiences may even help someone else.

Here is how Jeff says he answered those questions in the past:

- *Why are so many people suffering from depression and some of them are killing themselves?* I don't know, and I'm probably numb to it.

- *How do you feel about that?* I'm angry. I feel guilty.

- *What are you going to do about it?* I'm going to figure this out. I'm going to bring mental illness awareness and suicide prevention education to my community and beyond.

Why This Tool Is Needed

Think about all the people you know or come in contact with: your family members; the people you work with; the members of a faith institution, or club you belong to; the people you see walking along the sidewalk or riding mass transit; a restaurant full of people eating and seeming to have a good time. Now imagine that one out of every four of those people in the world, five in the U.S., is currently suffering from a mental illness (anxiety and depression being the most common) or will suffer from it at some point in their lives. You may see it in the faces of some, but most will never give any outward signs that are noticeable to the average observer. They will suffer unseen.

What you just imagined is true, which is a scary fact. But here's one that is even scarier: Nearly half of those who experience depression will never receive any professional treatment for it.[17] And untreated depression is 50 percent more likely to lead to suicide than treated depression is. No wonder so many suicides—90 percent of the total— are people who are victims of depression.

If you are a parent with a teenage child who has had some form of mental illness, there is a 16 percent chance that your child has had serious thoughts of taking his or her own life. There is an 11 percent possibility that he or she has actually come up with a plan to carry it out, and a 6 percent possibility that he or she will carry out an attempt. Those are alarming numbers, not only for parents but also for anyone who cares about the society we live in. This is the problem our society faces.

---

[17] "Key Substance Use and Mental Health Indicators in the United States: Results from the 2019 National Survey on Drug Use and Health," Substance Abuse and Mental Health Services Administration (SAMHSA), accessed April 21, 2021, www.samhsa.gov/data/sites/default/files/reports/rpt29393/2019NSDUHFRPDFWHTML/2019NSDUHFFR090120.htm.

This approach to mental health awareness and suicide prevention is not theory, nor is it just knowledge that gives understanding but still leaves people without practical steps to take. It actually works. As the MHF continues our work educating on the **be nice.** action plan and suicide prevention within the community, we've heard again and again how someone else took this action plan and used it to help *themselves and others.*

Once after giving a presentation on suicide awareness, a woman told me about how her son had long suffered from depression, partly from being bullied for years and being afraid even to go to school. He begged to stay home and would become physically ill at the thought of facing a peer group where he longed to be included in but that repeatedly and violently rejected him. His grades suffered, his health suffered, and his outlook on life grew dimmer and dimmer. "We felt helpless and prayed for a solution," she told me.

She and her husband heard about **be nice.** and attended an informational forum at the school. They learned about depression and how to recognize warning signs of suicidal tendencies—and gradually realized that the presenters were describing their son's symptoms. They had thought their biggest issue was a bully, but there was something deeper happening with their son, and they realized he might be thinking of taking his life. Learning the **be nice.** action plan helped them open the door to the needed conversation about suicide, and their son received the professional help he needed. They firmly believe that **be nice.** saved their son's life.

Not every story is about a dramatic, lifesaving encounter. Some are about the **be nice.** action plan subtly changing the climate of acceptance and creating a culture of understanding mental illness. After a training with local police officers, the county sheriff shared with me how positively the officers responded to the program and the action plan. One told him it really made him think about ways to help people when it came to mental health. Another said it should be in every school, and he was going to make sure his kids received this training. Police officers can be a tough audience, the sheriff said, yet every one of these officers saw the value in this action plan and wanted to do more to help spread it throughout West Michigan.

A grandmother of a student wrote to tell us that her adopted granddaughter got one of the Mental Health Foundation's **be nice.** shirts and wore it to school. She saw a boy crying in the bus line one day and went over to ask him what was wrong. He said that he and his younger brother had just been taken from their mother and put in foster care, and he was scared. "It will be okay," she said. "I was in foster care and separated from three of my sisters until we were adopted, and your foster mom is going to love you so much, and it will all be okay. I know you miss your mom because I missed mine too." This story proves you're never too young to learn about mental health. It also shows wearing the logo gave this young girl the confidence to help her fellow student. That conversation might not have happened if not for the **be nice.** action plan that helped create a climate of help and acceptance even among elementary school students.

These are examples of how **be nice.** is making a difference in the lives of real people and the schools, communities, organizations, and businesses they are involved in. And it isn't difficult to learn. You can begin incorporating it into your relationships and conversations even today.

A Place to Begin

Have you ever seen a change of behavior in someone in your family, workplace, place of worship, or circle of friends? Have you noticed someone who just doesn't seem to be happy at work? A child spending more than a usual amount of time alone and isolated in their bedroom? A friend growing more and more discouraged, bitter, or depressed? If so, what do you do? How do you address your concerns?

Each of these situations could represent typical ups and downs of life or they could signal a bigger problem. Without exploring them further, there's no way to know how to address them—or if addressing them is even necessary. But knowing how to explore them further is difficult. Many people don't know what questions to ask.

What about more critical situations when some sort of intervention is clearly necessary? Those are difficult too because asking the wrong questions could feel awkward or might even be perceived as offensive. Fear prevents many people from taking the next step, yet the next step could be a matter of life or death.

Imagine . . .

. . . receiving a call from a friend who says he or she is very depressed and doesn't know what to do;

. . . having a coworker tell you that another coworker privately shared thoughts about killing him- or herself;

. . . your son or daughter expressing concern that a friend has recently become very depressed, antisocial, and is behaving strangely—and seems on the verge of doing something rash.

These are real-life situations that, for most people, seem unlikely to happen to them so they never prepare for the next step. But if you were confronted with one of these situations, what would you do? The **be nice.** action plan provides a road map for circumstances like these.

This action plan does not qualify you to be a counselor or provide the professional help that people with mental health concerns need. Instead, it can help equip you to address that need with them and put them in touch with those who can provide those services.

chapter

7

notice

What Is Right and Different

Written by Christy Buck

Desmond was having trouble concentrating at work. In fact, he was having trouble in several areas of his life—difficulty sleeping, headaches, mood swings, and intense, ongoing stress. He had a good job, a new daughter, and a lot of situations in his life that, on the surface, appeared to be positive. But financial stresses, marital stress, and pressure from his supervisor were eroding his peace of mind. He turned inward—self-criticism, self-blame, and a vague sense that he couldn't handle it all. And to anyone who asked what was going on, all he could say was, "I don't know," "You don't know what it's like," or, "I just need a break."

After Desmond's loss of focus and energy contributed to several incidents at work—careless mistakes that put others in danger—his supervisor arranged a meeting with human resources to sort things out. His supervisor expected this meeting to end with Desmond's dismissal. He had had enough of what seemed to be Desmond's "irresponsibility."

The HR manager, Carol, listened to Desmond and his supervisor's explanations of the problem. Desmond had trouble putting words to his explanation, but he insisted that he was not being irresponsible or reckless. "I've just been tired," he said. "My kids have been keeping me up late."

Carol could sense more to the story than a loss of sleep. Desmond's fatigue and impaired concentration pointed to deeper concerns. She arranged for Desmond to take the rest of the day off and get some rest while she began making arrangements for him to get some professional help.

When Desmond returned to work, Chris, an observant and caring coworker, initiated a conversation.

"Why are you so tired?" Chris asked.

"Every night I go to sleep, but I can't stop these thoughts," Desmond answered.

"I get it. I've been there."

"What do you mean?"

"I've been there—and I've gotten out."

"How?"

"Therapy."

Desmond resisted the thought of therapy. He was used to handling everything on his own, and he wasn't sure he had time or the financial resources to go through with it. Still, he was at a crisis point. Something had to change.

Chris assured Desmond that therapy was worthwhile—and that

there were programs that would make the cost manageable, maybe even free.

Desmond overcame his resistance and had several therapy sessions that equipped him with positive coping skills. He was able to sleep again, stopped drinking, spent more time with his wife and family, and began to feel like his "old self" again. And he knows that none of these positive changes were likely to happen if not for Carol's and Chris's recognition of the warning signs and their willingness to address them.

This is the first step in implementing the **be nice.** action plan. Even when you cultivate an environment of respect, honor, and connection at a business or other organization, life's circumstances and the way a person handles them can lead to a crisis situation. This is one of those cases where the crisis was averted with intervention and the story had a happy ending.

Did you notice where that intervention began? The whole process of discovering Desmond's situation and helping him deal with it began because people noticed what was going on. Carol was an observant HR manager who knew to look for reasons behind the warning signs, but Chris had no background in counseling or social services. He worked at a manufacturing plant. He had been at the company for several years and simply took the time to know the people he worked with and notice changes in their attitudes and behaviors. He was willing to invite himself into a conversation, ask questions, and encourage Desmond to connect with people who could help him. His concern for his coworker required some proactive steps, but it wasn't difficult. He just needed some knowledge and the confidence that comes from it.

Because Carol and Chris noticed what was really going on, a man struggling with some painful situations and major stresses is alive and doing very well. He is able to enjoy his life, work, and relationships again.

A Culture of Noticing

The first step in noticing the warning signs in someone is not to look for what's wrong but to think about what's right. What is good and true and right about a person? What makes him or her special? What experiences, attributes, and perspectives make that person who he or she is? What characteristics, decisions, mannerisms, and expressions create a picture of that person's true nature? These are the attributes that make a person who they are.

Making those observations helps us in two ways. First, it enables us to appreciate others and affirm them. We naturally build up others when we're taking notice and letting them know the good things we see. It gives us an opportunity to simply **be nice** and acknowledge what we like and admire about that person. Maybe it's a common hobby, an interesting personality or life experience, or just the fact that he or she is a good person. Recognizing the positives is the first step.

The goal of the **be nice.** program is for this habit of noticing to be just that—a practice that creates a culture, not just a situational approach that looks for red flags and potential problems. Everyone's mental health is significantly shaped every day by the way other people treat them. Respect, affirmation, and encouragement are becoming rarer commodities in modern culture. Many of our attitudes and communications, especially those expressed online, have become toxic and divisive. People seem to be increasingly polarized and antagonistic toward each other. If we don't proactively make an effort to change the culture—even if only in our personal environment around us—mental health issues are only going to worsen. Noticing what's good and true and right in other people is the simplest, most effective way to address the problem of mental health. It isn't the only way—mental health for many people is at a more critical stage—but as we've seen, it begins upstream and creates an emotional climate that keeps many challenges from ever arising.

Making these observations about others helps us in another way too. In this context of respect and affirmation, it becomes natural to notice when a person has departed from his or her normal self. When people are suffering from the effects of depression, they are experiencing changes in their interests, their behavior, and their interactions. These changes may be visible or identifiable, but they can also remain pretty hidden within the mind of the sufferer. Still, there are often signs. Maybe someone who is typically well dressed starts coming in to work disheveled, or someone who is punctual is frequently late all of a sudden. They are unable to concentrate. Perhaps you notice someone who normally has a glass-half-full attitude suddenly taking on a glass-half-empty perspective. Minor or temporary fluctuations are usually not a concern, but drastic or long-term changes are. Signs that indicate someone may be in emotional pain and in need of help can include changes in personality, changes in social behavior, uncharacteristic emotions, or less attention to personal health and safety. These signs can fit generally into four main categories.

Words. Expressions of wanting to kill oneself, having no reason to live, being a burden to others, feeling trapped, or experiencing unbearable pain are strong signals that a person has reached a point of at least considering a way out. Frequent self-criticism or expressions of hopelessness or loneliness can be too. Sometimes these comments are subtle or veiled in unclear language, so clarifying what they mean can require some questions and follow-up. Clearly an expressed intention to kill oneself requires immediate action, but less obvious statements should lead to an immediate conversation as well.

Behavior. A person's risk of suicide is greater if a new behavior pattern arises (or an old one intensifies) related to a painful event, loss, or change. These behavioral changes can include the increased use of alcohol or drugs, exploring ways to take one's life (online searches, for example), acting recklessly, withdrawing from activities, quitting a favorite sport or hobby, isolating from family and friends, sleeping too much or too little, giving little attention to personal care and appearance, frequently missing school or work, visiting or calling people to say goodbye, giving away prized possessions, neglecting responsibilities, or demonstrating aggression. Again, some of these behaviors demand immediate intervention; all should prompt a conversation that includes direct questions about their intentions.

Emotions. People who are considering suicide often display one or more of these moods: hopelessness, feeling overwhelmed by circumstances, loss of interest, rage, irritability or agitation, humiliation, anxiety, guilt, frequent crying, loss of motivation, feeling worthless or burdensome, or sudden indifference or indecisiveness. None of these is necessarily a cause for alarm; everyone gets discouraged, irritable, or anxious at times. These are normal feelings in life. But if one or more of these significantly increases and persists, or if the person seems to have uncharacteristic difficulty controlling emotions, it could be a warning sign of something more serious. A conversation that asks what's going on beneath the surface and why the mood change has occurred is appropriate.

Physical health. Sickness and other changes in physical health can sometimes serve as visible signals of mental health issues. These might include fatigue or a lack of energy, either overeating or losing one's appetite, rapidly gaining or losing weight, headaches or other unexplained aches and pains, and a lack of hygiene or concern for personal appearance. Some of these can come from purely physical issues, which are worth exploring in their own right. But it's also worth exploring whether they are symptoms of emotional or psychological issues.

When someone exhibits one of these warning signs or noticeable behavioral changes for two weeks or longer, that person is possibly experiencing depression. Four or more noticeable changes within these categories that last for two weeks or longer dramatically increases the likelihood that this person is considering suicide. If you have taken notice of what is good and right about someone, even just an acquaintance, and observed what they typically like to do, you are equipped to notice the changes in his or her life.

notice is perhaps the most critical step in **be nice.** because it identifies the warning signs. As with almost any challenge in life, conditions must be identified or noticed before they can be addressed. Once you are armed with the awareness of these simple warning signs, you are prepared to take steps to improve or even save someone's life.

Noticing Isn't Always Easy

Lori Kroll lost her son Zach to suicide early in 2015 and has worked ever since to increase awareness and decrease the stigma of mental illness. She recalls the weekend her son took his life—how well things seemed to be going then, all the family and school activities that were going on and everything they were looking forward to. Beneath the surface of good times and enjoyable conversations, depression was stealing Zach's joy. He had been enduring silent pain for months.

Even as Zach contemplated ending his life, he was concerned about other people's happiness. But inside, he was overwhelmed by the pains and stresses no one knew about. Lori can recall no symptoms or signs. It was a sudden, horrifically tragic loss.

Not everyone exhibits warning signals. Depression is often referred to as a silent killer, and the main reason is because of the stigma attached to mental illness and a reluctance among many people to talk about it. Many who struggle with depression don't know how to express their feelings or ask for help. It can be very difficult to notice behavioral or emotional changes in a person who keeps their feelings inside.

Even so, no matter how subtle warning signs can be, they are usually there. People who die by suicide may exhibit one or more of them, either through what they say or what they do. And the more warning signs are present, the greater the risk of suicide there is.

It's important for "noticers" to take the initiative for addressing the signs and symptoms described above. People rarely volunteer that they are struggling with depression, partly for reasons we've discussed above (stigma, embarrassment, the sense that no one cares, etc.), and partly just from the nature of depression. Depressed people usually don't just wake up one day and seek help. As mentioned earlier, if you think back to the last time you had the flu or a bad cold, you can probably recall curling up on your bed or sofa and feeling helpless that there's nothing else you could do about this short-term illness. But imagine feeling that same sense of helplessness for months or even years. That's what a depressed person is dealing with, and the thought that someone could help them out of it is foreign. He or she may not even realize that any mood or behavior has changed because the feelings behind it have been there so long that they seem normal.

That's why it's so important to notice what is good and right about people before their behavior has changed. Sometimes people struggling with depression need someone to point out they are depressed—or at least that something out of the ordinary seems to be going on in their lives.

The characters in A *Million Little Things*, a TV drama series that began in 2017, were survivors of their friend's suicide. They kept wondering how they could not have seen the signs before it was too late. Why didn't they know their friend was hurting? Why didn't he get help? Some of them had spent hundreds of hours with this friend and didn't know what he was struggling with. They wondered if they even knew him at all. Only in retrospect did they begin to think about some of the subtle signs that were right there in front of them.

This is very common when someone dies by suicide. The people around that person wonder why they didn't see it coming. Eight out of ten people considering suicide give some sign of their intentions.

People who talk about suicide, threaten suicide, or call suicide crisis centers are thirty times more likely than average to kill themselves.[18] Only when we take time to notice what is good and right about people can we begin to see what is different or changing in their lives. When someone exhibits a change for two or more weeks, they may be wrestling with depression. If several identifiable changes occur, it's possible that suicidal ideation is somewhere beneath the surface.

The Power of Noticing

The nature of online conversations, the political tensions that exist in our world today, the fears provoked by current events and global crises . . . all contribute to a culture in which people criticize one another instead of uniting and affirming one another. Noticing what's good and right about people goes against that grain. It can be extremely and very positively countercultural. And it needs to be a philosophy of life.

Ideally, most people want to be better and would agree that this is one way to change the world. In reality, it's easy to get sucked into the divisive climate we live in. Noticing the good in people must become a very intentional art.

Everyone can be a noticer. We can't afford to allow ourselves to be desensitized by a divisive culture and its superficial values. We don't want to live in a world in which everyone minds his or her own business and doesn't pay attention to others—or worse, a world in which everyone is a potential adversary rather than a potential friend. Changing this culture begins with noticing, and it isn't complicated. Every one of

[18] "Suicide," Mental Health America, accessed April 21, 2021, www.mhanational.org/conditions/suicide.

us can make the mental shift to be a noticer.

It's a powerful shift. At one business that has made **be nice.** a part of its corporate culture, a presenter asked for a show of hands from those who had noticed recently what's good and right about someone and recently seen a change of behavior. A young salesperson in his early twenties raised his hand and told his story of noticing an elderly woman who was crying. She didn't seem like herself. So he asked if she was okay.

"No, I'm not," she said.

"Is there anything I can do?"

"No," she said, "but what you did for me just by recognizing that I'm not feeling well means the world to me. Thank you for helping me today."

There was no dramatic rescue, no need for intervention, no follow-up conversation. But the simple act of noticing and asking if someone was okay had such a positive effect that it changed her day—and his.

It isn't always easy or convenient to be a noticer. In the biblical story of the Good Samaritan, two people passed by a wounded man lying beside the road and chose not to "notice" him. They saw, but they didn't want to get involved. They lived with a mind-your-own-business mentality, just as many people do today. But one went out of his way not only to notice but to help, even though helping was inconvenient and costly. This is the only way to create the kind of culture in which mental disorders like depression and suicidal thinking become rarer.

You can probably think of some obstacles to living out this role of noticing the good and right about people and the ways they depart from their typical attitudes and behavior. Maybe this requires some new ways of thinking that take some time to develop, especially if you're a private person and generally keep to yourself. Perhaps you get very busy and distracted, as most of us tend to do. Or maybe you've just never recognized the need. But contributing to this environment of noticing, respecting, and affirming will benefit your life as much as it benefits others. It may not feel convenient at first, but it is very worthwhile.

You can't change the whole culture, but you can change your piece of it. And you can create ripple effects that profoundly affect other lives. Whether you want the responsibility or not, your words and actions have the power to benefit the mental health of people around you. And by noticing the good and true and right in others—and when they don't seem like themselves anymore—you can take the next step to invite.

chapter
8

invite

Yourself to Start a Conversation

Written by Christy Buck

I was teaching a series of **be nice.** sessions in a public school, which the Mental Health Foundation often does, and during one of the sessions when the class was watching a movie on suicide, one student got up and walked out.

I had noticed her demeanor in previous sessions. She would sit on the edges of the classroom, often wore a hood over her head, usually had her arms crossed and her head down, and never made eye contact with me as the presenter. I could tell she was listening intently, but she didn't want to show interest. Sitting in a dark room for the movie that day probably made this avoidance easier for her, but I could still tell something was wrong. At one point I noticed she was crying. Not too long into the movie, she left the room and stayed out until the end. Once it was over, she walked back in to get her books and started packing up her things.

Even though I didn't know much about this student personally, noticing her mood and behavior was not difficult. But that's just the first step, and I felt like I needed to invite myself into a conversation with her. I walked over and addressed her by name—even though she had not participated outwardly, I wanted to show her I cared and I was concerned by simply taking the time to remember her name—and told her I'd love to talk to her for a minute.

"I don't have time right now," she told me.

"I understand, but there's something really important I need to speak to you about." Then I went directly into the action plan. "I noticed that you started to tear up during the movie, and you got up and left the room. I don't know much about you outside of this class, but I can see that you're listening intently to the lessons *(this is pointing out the right/good)*. Today when we watched the movie on suicide prevention, you didn't want to listen anymore and walked out *(this is pointing out the different)*. So I'm just going to ask you right now. Are you thinking about suicide?"

"No, I'm not thinking about that. I would never do that."

"Okay, that's good. What do you mean by, 'I would never do that'?"

"I would never put a family through that."

"Yeah, that's really hard on a family," I said. "Do you know a family where that happened?"

"My dad killed himself."

Wow. My heart just went out to her. For weeks, we had been talking about something that was still extremely painful for her, an open wound, that she was trying to cope with.

She had opened up to me, so I invited myself to further the conversation. I found out she was in second grade when she suddenly lost her dad, and on the day of his death she was shuttled off to school and never received any kind of counseling or professional help. It was an unimaginably traumatic experience for her. We know that trauma has a major influence on mental illness, and researchers keep learning more and more about how major trauma can have long-term effects on a young person.

She was now a freshman in high school, her father's death had been at least six or seven years earlier, and she had not been equipped with the tools to heal.

"Okay, well, now is the time for counseling," I told her. "Would you be willing to go to the counseling office with me and see if we can connect you with someone?"

She agreed, and we visited the counseling center. That day she was connected to professionals in the community who could help her. Right away, the counselors found some things that could help her move forward. She played in the school band, so she was encouraged to stay plugged in to that and other school activities, continue to pursue her interests outside of school, and to remain involved. Having a sense of connection to school is a major protective factor for young people. Although the nature of these illnesses makes it difficult, it is so important for people struggling with depression or anxiety to keep doing things that connect them to others and engage their minds. Moving forward in this direction was the beginning of a journey of healing for her, and it started with a simple conversation.

As you can see from this story, noticing is just the first step. The next step is to invite yourself into a conversation with that person so you can begin to explore what's going on. This is the first step of engagement—having a conversation. It isn't just going to "come up." You have to invite yourself into it.

Initiate a Two-Way Invitation

Many cases of depression go untreated if they are not noticed by a loved one or peer. The shame, stigma, and a lack of knowledge make people reluctant to talk about depression, anxiety, suicidal thoughts, and other forms of mental illness. Depression can be an isolating illness. It's important to invite yourself into someone's life with love and care because they may need someone else to take the initiative.

It's important to use "I" statements instead of "you" statements. "I've noticed you're not enjoying the things you usually love to do." "I've noticed you haven't seemed like yourself lately." "I've always enjoyed your positive attitude, and I've been missing it." "I'm concerned that you aren't making it into work on time recently." All of these comments make yourself the subject and ward off any misperceptions about intent.

After you've expressed your concerns, you can follow up your statement by summing up and turning the invitation around to them. You've invited yourself into the conversation; now it's your turn to be a listening ear and invite them to respond. "I'm concerned because you don't seem like yourself lately. I've noticed you're coming to work late, you haven't responded when I've reached out with text messages, and you haven't been going to the gym. Are you okay?"

"You" statements sometimes come across as an accusation, as

if the behavior is the sole issue. "I" statements take all the accusation out of the conversation and major on your concern for the person's well-being, not your expectations for how he or she should behave. Be careful to make sure your "I" statements are coming from you alone. "I've heard that you have not been yourself lately" is not really an "I" statement; it's a "someone else" statement that makes it clear that the person has been the subject of conversation. It's hearsay, and it only adds to whatever stigma and shame the person might feel. While you may feel safety in numbers by using a "we've noticed" statement, it's more important that the person you're approaching feels safe and knows you're someone they can trust.

By having a conversation like this, you may feel like you're taking a big risk. By noticing someone's changes in behavior and initiating a conversation, you are sharing your love and care in a non-judgmental, non-confrontational way. There's nothing offensive in this approach; in fact, most people open up when they know someone cares. People usually respond positively.

Inviting yourself to have this conversation with someone who is struggling with depression can be a lifechanging moment for that person. People in crisis usually do not have the capacity to seek help on their own—not because they don't want to, but because they don't know where to go, who to talk to, or what to say. They face a number of potential barriers: pride, social status, personal history, historical biases, need for approval, fear of disrupting the status quo, and many more. One conversation from a person who cares can overcome any or all of those barriers.

Now, you may have made it much easier for the person you're

concerned about to accept the invitation you've given them to open up and share what's on their mind. Listen carefully and compassionately. This is not the time to give advice. It's time to hear what's going on. You have invited yourself into this person's inner life, even if only for a moment.

If the conversation reveals some signs of depression or anxiety, take it a little further. You've initiated the conversation with what you have noticed, and now you need to follow up.

Key Questions

- *Is there anything going on that's brought about these changes?* Asking this question can give you a deeper understanding of situations the person is possibly dealing with. The answer could be they don't know how to deal with a stressful life situation, and you could offer your help.

- *How long have you been feeling this way?* This will give you information about the length of these feelings. Two weeks or longer calls for concern.

- *Have you talked to anyone about how you're feeling?* This will give you a better idea of whether or not their family or someone they trust is aware of what's going on. This also lets you know whether or not they are currently in or have been in treatment.

- *Is there anyone or anything that has helped you in the past with these feelings?* This question gives you a sense of whether or not this person has internal coping skills to manage the concern or situation, and clues to who you can involve outside of this conversation setting.

Remember you're not a counselor. You're just trying to find out what's going on in this person's mind. But it does help to know what's really going on. Sometimes fear, anger, or other emotions prove to be exaggerated or based on faulty reasoning. This brief conversation can demonstrate your concern and set the stage, if necessary, for the direct questions to come.

When Mental Illness Hits Home

Inviting yourself into a conversation with a friend or coworker is different from initiating a conversation at home. It brings up deeper and more personal emotions; requires an extraordinary amount of energy, engagement, and compassion; and can feel threatening at times to your own sense of well-being. When your partner, child, or another family member is depressed, the dynamics of conversations change, and this can be difficult and oftentimes an enormous responsibility to manage on a daily basis. It can feel very heavy and exhausting. As challenging as it can be, however, it's very important in that context to maintain a relationship of love, comfort, and support for your loved one—and to get the love, comfort, and support you need for yourself from other sources.

When you live with someone, you are likely to notice changes in moods and behaviors that other people don't. You may be the first line of defense in addressing a mental illness. While it's never a good idea to try to diagnose a loved one's mental health, you can go a bit deeper than most people in asking questions about how the person's symptoms are affecting home life. Even if you already know the answers to the questions, just asking them establishes an environment of empathy and lets your loved one know he or she is important to you. Because of your role in your loved one's life, you can be a significant part of his or her recovery from depression, an anxiety disorder, or other emotional conditions.

In addition to asking the general questions about what is causing the change in attitude or behavior you've noticed, your relationship puts you in a position to explore more specifically things like sleeping and eating patterns, feelings of fatigue, personal satisfaction and enjoyment in activities and responsibilities, and other questions that might reveal how this person feels about life.

While everyone feels a little down from time to time, these questions may help distinguish between those typical experiences and the possibility of clinical depression. If it seems to be just a temporary "rough spot," ask your loved one how you can help him or her get through this difficult season or what changes you can make together to help him or her feel better. Think back to any other similar experiences and ask what helped with those. You are much more relationally connected with this person than you would be with a coworker or friend, so spend some time talking through shared experiences and possible solutions.

Use words that suggest a team effort rather than any that might make your loved one feel guilty, overly responsible, or alone in the situation. This is a "we" conversation, not a "you" conversation. Whatever it turns up, you're going to walk through it with them. Above all, resist any impulse to try to fix the situation, artificially "cheer them up," suggest that this will go away soon, or minimize the seriousness of these feelings. Be supportive and understanding. Don't react negatively if you encounter resistance; the first response to a loved one's concern is sometimes negative or even hostile. Just listen, encourage, seek help, and walk through this valley together.

If your conversation does reveal something more serious than a discouraging season, take the steps in the next two chapters to challenge and empower. Walk with your loved one with compassion and commitment, not as someone who needs to manage the situation but as a facilitator to get the professional help that is needed.

In the meantime, take care of yourself. A loved one's depression can feel like a heavy weight, and it's important to give yourself permission to seek support and manage your own needs. Prioritize your well-being by actively working to avoid burnout. Your emotional strength is important both for you and the one you are trying to help. Get enough sleep, eat well, exercise regularly, talk to people who have gone through similar experiences, and, if needed, seek out professional resources to help you.

Some families even "invite" before noticing. Letting your loved ones know that every member in the family is committed to open conversations at any time about having suicidal thoughts lets them know that the family is a safe, welcoming, compassionate place. This commitment has to be genuine; everyone, especially children and teenagers, needs to know that no one is going to panic or overreact if they admit to having thoughts about harming themselves. But this kind of family pact can express love and concern before any need for intervention is ever noticed or even arises. Proactive conversations like this are a great way to address a potential crisis when no one is feeling any pressure or discomfort over the issue.

An Act of Compassion

Inviting yourself to have a conversation with someone about the changes you've been seeing in his or her behavior, attitude, mood, or physical appearance is where your concern shifts from mere observance to meaningful action. It is the first practical step you can take to get this person the help he or she needs. The "n" in **be nice.** represents the knowledge you gain from noticing people. Now the "i" puts that knowledge to use as you share it and enter into a conversation.

When you reach out and invite yourself to show someone you care, it instills the feeling of hope. Think of the compassion we outwardly show to people who are struggling with a physical illness or ailment. Remember, people with a mental illness feel psychological pain and need compassion too.

challenge

The Stigma

Written by Christy Buck

Todd was successful at his job and had good friends. But he was also stressed at work and lonely. For about a year—ever since his fiancée was killed in a car accident while he was driving—he had not seemed like himself. He was socially uncomfortable, had ongoing conflict with some of his coworkers, and even wondered if anyone would really care if he died. He felt hopeless and covered his feelings with awkward attempts at humor, alcohol, and avoiding normal activities.

Todd's boss noticed and invited herself to have a conversation with him. She pointed out that since Todd had taken some time off after the accident, he had called in sick seventeen times, had skipped the office Christmas party and company picnic, and was expressing some very negative thoughts about himself. She pointed out that even though Todd's coworkers all seemed to like him, he still thought they might not care if he were gone.

"I'm concerned enough that I have to ask," she said. "Have you had thoughts of suicide?"

"No, it's not like that," Todd told her. "I mean, it's only been a year, and I just miss her so much."

Grief in the aftermath of a tragic loss is normal and understandable, a common human experience that does not have to lead to depression. But Todd's boss knew he was exhibiting something more than normal symptoms of grief. "There is hope," she assured him. "And the first step is talking to someone. Can you do that for me?"

At first, Todd wasn't sure. He knew he wasn't doing well, but he didn't think he needed therapy—that was for people who have really "serious" issues. He thought he was just struggling a bit and could manage it on his own.

Todd knows now what his boss had noticed in his behavior. He was experiencing depression. His boss invited herself to have a conversation with him and was not afraid to ask a difficult question. She challenged him to get help to overcome his sense of stigma by reassuring him that therapy was nothing to be embarrassed about. And Todd responded well. He challenged himself to go and stick with the sessions. He learned to empower himself with positive coping skills, joined a grief support group at his church, stopped drinking to mask his pain, and reengaged with some of his friends.

Todd wasn't bothered that his boss asked him if he was thinking about suicide. "That was actually a relief," he said. He knew someone cared. He still misses his fiancée, and he still faces challenges every day, but feels like he has his life—and his hope—once again.

You've probably noticed in this story and the others we've shared so far that they have the potential to pivot around a critical question. The conversation begins with concern over some observations, but in many cases it leads to that question. Then, based on the answer, it usually moves on from there with some specific steps. It's a direct question, and not always comfortable to ask, but it reveals vital information: Is this person thinking about suicide? The primary purpose of the conversation is to get an answer to that question and know how to help this person move forward toward help and healing.

Stigma Is the Number One Reason People Don't Seek Help

The word *stigma* originally referred to a visible mark made by a pointed object—a kind of brand that marked someone, often with a negative meaning. When the word began to be used in English, it usually meant the kind of mark or stain that cannot be seen. We still use it today with negative connotations: the stigma of homelessness, or the stigma of being overweight . . . or the stigma of mental illness.

No matter how much we try to normalize mental illness as one of many illnesses a person can have, it still carries a stigma. It is not discussed in the same way physical illnesses are, even though there are some very physical aspects of mental illnesses. The person struggling is oftentimes embarrassed by the symptoms that accompany their illness and this lowers their self-esteem. Because of the invisibility of some symptoms and the behavioral component of others, people with mental illness are often stigmatized by others—so much so that they may live in fear of losing a job or a relationship.

This fear is so strong that some who have already lost a job will still put on their office clothes every morning and pull out of their driveways to avoid neighbors' suspicions and the stigma that inevitably follows. Stigma compels people to keep up false appearances.

That is one of the many reasons that overcoming depression is not easy. It is an enormous challenge for the people who struggle with the disease, and it requires those around them to look beyond appearances, notice what's going on, and accept the challenge to take the next step.

Jeff has shared that if he could go back and ask his brother Wayne the right questions, he would ask him why he didn't put his boat in the water during a whole summer, or why he didn't make any plans for a ski trip over the winter—things he typically did every year. I would ask him why he quit enjoying a drink on occasion, whether it was a positive health decision or an inability to enjoy the things he used to do. Why did he lose thirty pounds or quit going out to dinner with friends? Some behaviors can be perfectly typical for most people, but if they are not typical for the person you're concerned about, then they represent an alarming change. After being educated in the **be nice.** action plan, these are now behaviors Jeff recognizes as warning signs.

If you've noticed the warning signs and invited yourself to have a loving and caring conversation about your observations of their change in behavior, it is time to personally challenge yourself to be ready and able to ask a difficult question: "Are you thinking of killing yourself?" Not every conversation will lead to that point, but if you've already noticed significant behavioral changes in the person and expressed your concerns, it's important you ask this question.

Don't put it off for a "better" time when someone's life is at stake. There is no better time. Having that conversation and working up the nerve to ask that question can be difficult, but it could be lifesaving.

Remember, one of the greatest myths about suicide is that asking the question will put the idea into someone's mind, when, in fact, asking someone directly if they are thinking suicidal thoughts is an act of compassion and a potentially lifesaving opportunity. This could be the first time they have the opportunity to talk about how they are thinking of or feeling about suicide.

In a study of nearly lethal suicide attempts in Houston, Texas, 153 survivors thirteen to thirty-four years old were asked how much time there was between the time they decided to attempt suicide and when they actually attempted. One in four deliberated for less than five minutes. Seven out of ten said less than one hour, and nine out of ten deliberated for less than one day.[19] For this reason, asking the question and opening the dialogue for that conversation could be lifesaving.

Notice the wording of this question. It is not framed negatively, as in, "You're not thinking of killing yourself, are you?" Nor is it vague, as in, "Are you thinking of hurting yourself?" Those are not the same questions, and they allow too much room to skirt the issue. "Are you thinking of killing yourself?" or "Have you had thoughts of suicide?" leaves little room for avoidance. If the answer is any form of "yes" or even "maybe," follow up with another question: "Do you have a plan?" The answer may indicate how far the person has thought things through and whether some harmful action is imminent. But any suggestion that

---

[19] T. R. Simon, A. C. Swann, K. E. Powell, L. B. Potter, M. Kresnow, and P. W. O'Carroll, "Characteristics of Impulsive Suicide Attempts and Attempters," SLTB 32 supp. (2001): 49–59.

suicidal thoughts or a plan of action are present, no matter how far they have progressed, is an indication that it's time to get help.

The reason these critical questions are so important to ask is that you want to give your friend or loved one the opportunity to express his or her real feelings and thoughts. The depressed person with suicidal ideation has been living with a secret, and now someone has noticed it. Those questions uncover it. Once the silence has been broken, it is no longer just an internal conversation. This bold questioning coming from someone who cares—and who will not be judgmental about the answer—may offer quite a bit of relief.

Again, if the answer is any form of "yes" (like "maybe," "occasionally," "it's crossed my mind," etc.), then it's time for someone to take action—for help to be offered, support to be given, and next steps to be planned out. In other words, it's time for you and the person who has been struggling to be empowered.

In the stories we've shared in the last two chapters, this question has led to negative answers. Neither Todd nor the student Christy spoke with in class said they had had suicidal thoughts. But regardless of the answer, this question does not end the discussion. There is still more to talk about—we'll get to that in the next chapter—and those conversations will be different based on the responses to the question. In every case, the person who is struggling needs some professional assistance to handle the thoughts, feelings, and issues they are dealing with.

Not all of these conversations end with a nice resolution and everything on the right track. You'll find that to be the case when you implement this action plan. People's lives are open-ended, and just because a season of uncertainty seems to have been resolved doesn't mean similar struggles won't come up again later. That means, of course, that the "noticing" step in this plan never really ends. This step is always recycling. It's always important to be observant and notice the changes and fluctuations in people's lives. The other steps are always on the table too, if and when they might be needed. But your role as a "lifeguard" in these critical times is exactly what is needed in the moment. Every time you implement this plan, you are providing a vital and compassionate service.

A Compassionate Question

A man who had learned the **be nice.** action plan noticed some changes in his father's life. The father had recently retired, and like many retirees, he was leaving much of what he had known. He was moving away from his professional life but not sure what he was moving into. He was acting as if he had lost his purpose and was no longer doing the things he normally loved to do. He used to go fishing all the time and had not gone even once since his retirement.

The son invited himself into a conversation with his father and walked him through the things he had noticed. They had a loving, compassionate conversation. And then the son asked his father directly, "Are you thinking of killing yourself?"

"No, I wouldn't do that," his father said, surprised that his son would ask such a thing. But then he followed up with appreciation for his son's concern. "I love you for asking that. Thank you for caring about me."

The "challenge" question can seem awkward and surprising

because most people aren't used to talking about such things. The feelings that go with depression are often kept beneath the surface, treated as a very private matter, and few people want to intrude on such private thoughts. But if those thoughts and feelings become dangerous or threatening, they need to be brought to the surface. And the best way to do that is to ask.

As with the father in the story above, the question may be a little startling. But it comes from a heart of compassion, and most people understand and appreciate the concern.

The only way to destigmatize mental illness is to stop treating it as if it carries a stigma and start talking about it the same way we talk about physical illness. The goal of this chapter and of the "challenge" step of the **be nice.** action plan is to encourage just that. Noticing the changes in a person's life and inviting yourself into a conversation about them leads us to a point of asking the tough questions, and this action plan equips us to ask them. The knowledge and confidence to do so could save a life.

empower

Yourself and Others with Education and Resources

Written by Christy Buck

Abby stood at her locker, nervously practicing for the presentation she was about to make in her English class. When the bell rang, she made her way to the classroom and sat down. Tense, anxious, and hoping with all her heart that she would not stutter this time, she waited for the teacher to call her up to present her paper.

She didn't have to wait long. The teacher called on her first, and she walked tentatively up to the podium. About thirty seconds into her presentation—having only stumbled over a few words—she looked down at her notes and realized they weren't hers. She had not noticed before class began that the student sitting behind her had switched them with another paper as a prank. Nor did she realize, as she went back to her desk and fumbled through all of her notebooks, that the prankster was recording the whole scene. Abby's time ran out, she couldn't complete her assignment, and she went home feeling humiliated.

Abby isolated herself and slept most of the weekend. Her father noticed something was wrong, asked her if she was still taking her medication, and told her he loved her. She appreciated the support but still dreaded school. As she filled her backpack to leave that morning, she saw something horrifying on her phone—a video of her disastrous presentation, complete with mocking comments from her classmates. She wished she never had to go back. She just wanted to disappear.

Sitting in English class again, waiting for the teacher to begin, Abby felt a tap on her arm. The student next to her had something to say—*another person who wants to make fun of me*, she must have thought.

"Hey, Abby. I know you don't know me," the classmate said. "But I saw the video they took of you, and what they did was wrong. Some people just don't know how hurtful they're being. If you want to go to the counseling office after class, I'll go with you."

"I don't know," Abby said. She was having trouble making friends, had been embarrassed in front of a class, and now—in front of the whole school, thanks to a social media post—wasn't sure what a school counselor could do to fix any of it.

"They can help," her classmate said. "It's why they're here."

Abby and her new friend went to the school office after class and talked with a counselor. They talked about a lot of things that were going on in her life and about the ways thoughtless comments and behaviors of others can add to the stresses and fears that are already going on in someone's mind.

"That day when a stranger decided to reach out, they followed the **be nice.** action plan," Abby says. "And in those simple steps, they saved my life."

In implementing the **be nice.** action plan, it's important to empower the person who is struggling to take the steps to get help. That's true regardless of whether he or she is having suicidal thoughts. If genuine warning signs are present and depression seems to be part of the problem, the causes need to be addressed.

You've seen that in every story we've shared so far. Desmond needed Chris to encourage him to get the professional help he needed. The student who had never gotten counseling after her father's suicide needed therapy to be able to deal with all the emotions and scars that came from that traumatic experience. Todd needed someone to recognize his depression, ask the direct question about suicidal thoughts, and work with him to set up an appointment. Abby needed someone to recognize her struggles and go with her in taking the next steps to talk to someone about them. None of these deep emotional issues is manageable for someone alone, and people who are struggling with ongoing anxiety, stress, and depression are not in a great position to take the initiative in getting help. The conversation needs to lead to some specific next steps.

Suicide Prevention Involves Everyone

A person's chance of developing a mental illness and being at risk for suicide depends on many factors that can be categorized in two ways: risk factors and protective factors. Effective prevention must focus on both. If we're going to take specific steps to reduce the rate of suicide, we need to reduce risk factors and amplify protective factors through empowerment.

We discussed risk factors in chapter 3—depression, family history, abuse, social isolation, and many more. But protective factors are different. They are personal or environmental characteristics that, as the name suggests, help protect people from suicide. Empowering people involves connecting and equipping them with the services, relationships, values, and skills they need to protect against mental illness and suicide. Major protective factors for suicide include:

- Effective behavioral health care

- Connectedness to individuals, family, community, and social institutions

- Life skills (including problem solving skills and coping skills, ability to adapt to change, self-awareness)

- Self-esteem and a sense of purpose or meaning in life

- Cultural, religious, or personal beliefs that discourage suicide

It's important to make sure that the first of these, effective behavioral health care, is available for people at risk for suicide as a key component of prevention. Here's what that involves:

- Treatment for suicide risk should be evidence-based and focus directly on suicidal thoughts and behaviors along with treatment for mental and/or substance use disorders.

- Every community should offer multiple levels of care so people at risk have ready access to the best available care in the least restrictive setting.

- Health and behavioral health care organizations should establish care pathways for patients with suicide risk to ensure they receive follow-up and referral services in a timely manner—particularly during high-risk periods.

- The integration of primary care and behavioral health care must be promoted to increase access to behavioral health services in primary care settings.

- Key stakeholders must collaborate to expand the capacity of community-level behavioral health and crisis services to meet the demand for these services and promote care in the least restrictive setting.[20]

In other words, this is a communal effort, which points to the second protective factor: connection at both personal and broader social levels. Personal relationships and social support are key protective factors against suicide. Positive and supportive social relationships and community connections can help buffer the effects of risk factors in people's lives. Programs and practices that promote social connectedness and support are one element of a comprehensive approach to suicide prevention.

In 2011, the Centers for Disease Control and Prevention (CDC) adopted promoting connectedness as its strategic direction for preventing suicidal behavior. It defined connectedness as "the degree to which a person or group is socially close, interrelated, or shares resources with other persons or groups." This connectedness can include family members, friends, neighbors, coworkers, etc.; commu-

---

[20] Suicide Prevention Resource Center (SPRC).

nity organizations and institutions like schools, churches, etc.; and workplaces.[21]

The Suicide Prevention Resource Center (SPRC) suggests that activities in educational institutions that help students increase and strengthen their social networks and connections are an important protective factor.

Life skills—the ability to manage life events, especially adverse ones—are also a key protective factor for suicide and include critical thinking, stress management, conflict resolution, problem-solving, and coping skills. Activities that enhance these skills can help people as they face new challenges, such as economic stress, divorce, physical illness, and aging. Resilience, a related concept, includes traits like a positive self-concept and optimism. This is sometimes described as the ability to adapt to stress and adversity. Building life skills and resilience is a necessary part of a comprehensive approach to suicide prevention.

Targeting only one context when addressing a person's protective factors is unlikely to be successful, because people don't exist in isolation. For example:

- In relationships, parental involvement is an example of a protective factor.

- In communities, protective factors could include the availability of faith-based resources and after-school activities.

- In society, protective factors in this context might include hate-crime laws or policies limiting the availability of alcohol.

---

[21] Centers for Disease Control and Prevention (CDC), "Strategic Direction for the Prevention of Suicidal Behavior: Promoting Individual, Family, and Community Connectedness to Prevent Suicidal Behavior," accessed April 21, 2021, www.cdc.gov/ViolencePrevention/pdf/Suicide_Strategic_Direction_Full_Version-a.pdf.

Protective factors also tend to have a cumulative effect on the development—or reduced development—of behavioral health issues. Young people with multiple protective factors are at a reduced risk of physical and mental health problems.

All of these are important. To take to the next level the protective factors that our communities should consider, where we can make a marked impact on how people think, act, and feel, we need to be aware of the impact mental illness has on families, schools, faith institutions, and workplaces. Then we can implement the **be nice.** action plan to notice what is right and good about someone. A person may seem "just fine" but be struggling with a mental illness and perhaps even suicidal ideation. When we provide our communities with the protective factors noted above, we will see a mentally healthier and happier society.

Your Empowerment and Theirs

Even as the number of incidences of mental illness continues to grow, resources remain quite limited, but good ones do exist. To empower yourself or an individual to get help is to empower them to take the first steps by connecting them with existing resources and opportunities to receive professional care.

Now that you know how to notice, invite, and challenge, it is time to empower. Through this step, you can serve as a connecting point between someone managing depression or another mental illness and protective factors that a person might explore, which can include access to services; like talk therapy, medication, or exercise, among many others; utilizing these services; and being in a supportive environment. After taking every other step in the action plan, you can now become a bridge to practical and effective solutions.

At this point, you can be considered a protective factor. When you implement this part of the action plan, you are investing yourself even further in this person's life. You are no longer a detached observer. At this point, you are more than a comforting voice. empower yourself to support them on their journey to better mental health.

This doesn't mean you have to check in every day or that you are responsible for managing their treatment, but it could involve some follow-up communication. To give someone help is to give someone hope. Hope reassures us that recovery is possible. It's the common denominator in every kind of recovery—physical, mental, or otherwise. Hope makes healing and recovery possible.

People who have opened up and become vulnerable in sharing their personal struggles with you will more than likely agree to seek professional treatment. No matter how they answer this question, you should have resources available at that time including contact information for primary care physicians, inpatient care facility, clinicians, and help lines. A "yes" answer to your direct question in the "challenge" step should prompt an immediate search for the empowerment step. That may begin at the emergency room of a hospital, where trained staff are accustomed to administering intake assessments and recommending a course of action. An even more immediate first step would be calling the National Suicide Prevention Lifeline at 1-800-273-8255, which offers free and confidential crisis counseling and emotional support twenty-four hours a day for people in distress. The Lifeline is part of a national network of more than 150 local crisis centers that adhere to best practices and comply with national standards. If you know of other available resources in the community, like a program at work or at school or crisis counseling services through a faith organization, you can begin there. The important thing is to take action.

Approaches like psychotherapy are more accessible to more people than ever. Sources for help and treatment can be found at www.samhsa.gov, a national registry for mental health treatment resources assembled by the Substance Abuse and Mental Health Services Administration (SAMHSA).

A growing and acceptable form of care is telehealth or teletherapy. It is a form of video conferencing allowing psychiatrists and therapists to provide services to patients outside of the office, for example, at the patient's home or workplace. It also provides the opportunity for consultation with family members, teachers, and other providers involved in the patient's care. Surveyed patients participating in telemedicine say they are very satisfied with the care they are receiving and that they feel telemedicine is a reliable form of practice. In addition, they find that they are able to keep their appointments on a more regular basis.[22]

A study published in the *Journal of Clinical Psychiatry* comparing in-office treatment to treatment via telepsychiatry indicated, "There were no statistically significant differences between study groups for symptoms, quality of life, and patient satisfaction . . . there is a strong hypothesis that videoconference-based treatment obtains the same results as face-to-face therapy and that telepsychiatry is a useful alternative."[23]

---

[22] Life Stance Health.

[23] Francisca García-Lizana and Ingrid Muñoz-Mayorga, "What about Telepsychiatry? A Systematic Review," *Journal of Clinical Psychiatry* 12, no. 2 (2010): https://doi.org/10.4088/PCC.09m00831whi.

As we have seen, shame prevents many from seeking professional help, and cost—even just the expense of co-pays and deductibles, with some insurance plans—may be prohibitive, depending on a person's income and budget. Not being able to afford treatment may add to the perceived shame that already exists, and many people never make it past the first step to seek the care they need. But many communities have providers who can offer subsidized or reduced-cost counseling services. Copays are sometimes determined on an income-based sliding scale, resulting in extremely low costs per session for clients who cannot afford regular rates. Free online mental health screening can provide a quick assessment for anyone who needs it.[24]

Empowering people to get help is not just a matter of providing helpful information. It may require some accountability and follow-up. It may mean walking with them through the process and helping them overcome obstacles along the way.

Now that you know the action plan, you have a few starting points. When you connect someone with professional services, they can be assessed and given recommendations for treatment. You serve primarily as a catalyst for getting started.

---

[24] See www.mentalhealthscreeing.org, for example.

PART FOUR

God, please use me to help others.

A Time for Action

PART FOUR

God, please use me to help others.

A Time for Action

The steps of the **be nice.** action plan that we've covered in the last few chapters are individually applied. These are steps each person can take to build the confidence to take action when it comes to a crisis situation.

But what can we do on a larger scale? How can we bring this tool into a community? How do we get it into schools, faith communities, businesses, government agencies, and other social organizations? How do we overcome the institutional obstacles that typically arise when new initiatives are introduced?

That can be a challenge. Most people, including leaders and administrators in a position to scale this tool up into wider use, can appreciate the need for it but may not have the time or resources to implement it. Those who do, though, are finding it well worth the time and effort. It has transformed the culture of businesses, schools, and communities, improving relationships, morale, and productivity, and often saving money. It is making a significant impact.

The following chapters look at some of the ways **be nice.** can be utilized both by individuals and in communities, as well as some of the challenges in doing so. It will require a broad effort from many sectors of society, not just from a few specialists and those who have been touched by suicide's effects. We have seen the need in part 1 and shown how it can be met at an individual level in parts 2 and 3, and we begin this section with some examples of personal application. There's no reason for **be nice.** not to have a much greater impact in our world. In the following pages, let's explore how.

be nice.
in Action

Written by Jeff Elhart and Christy Buck

This approach to suicide prevention has changed relationships; saved lives; and transformed the atmosphere of business, places of worship, schools, and other organizations. If there were room, this book could be filled with example after example. Here are a few that show how it can be used in a variety of contexts.

●

"Amy," a high school senior, was at a church camp when a fellow student pulled her aside and shared some thoughts of harming herself.

"No one would care if I wasn't here anymore," she said. "I'm just tired of trying to be perfect all the time."

Amy asked if her friend had talked to anyone about these feelings or gotten any counseling for them. Her friend told her that she had not—and didn't want to.

Amy had already noticed some of the changes going on in her friend's life. She was typically confident and energetic, but she had become quieter and more reserved. She had been crying easily and just didn't seem like herself. Now Amy knew how much her friend was struggling, and the idea that an intelligent student and talented athlete could think such negative thoughts about herself was very concerning.

Amy knew the **be nice.** action plan and invited her friend to go to the guidance office together next time they were at school, but the friend repeatedly rejected the idea. She didn't want help or even think she really needed it.

So Amy challenged herself to get out of her comfort zone. She knew the stakes could be high—that her friend was in a more dangerous situation than she would admit—and she knew it was important to take every threat seriously. The thought of losing her friend to suicide was terrifying. She was determined to connect her friend with a trusted adult.

At Amy's insistence—and her direct questions—the friend went with her to visit the school's counselors that Monday, and they connected her with a professional counselor who could talk through her thoughts and feelings with her. Amy credits the **be nice.** action plan with giving her the knowledge and confidence to know what to do in this situation and to overcome the stigma involved in getting her friend into treatment.

●

Travis was kicked out of a test for cheating and told to take it at a later time. He acted like it didn't bother him, and in reality, it wasn't the biggest of his concerns. Those surfaced later as he was hanging out with his best friends. While they played video games, he put his headphones on to listen to music, had a few drinks, and pulled out his phone to look through some pictures of his ex-girlfriend, Stacy.

When Travis saw a picture of Stacy with her new boyfriend, he flipped. "Did you ever even care for me?" he texted her.

A few minutes later, her response lit up his screen. "What's your problem, Travis??? It's been seven months. And you're the one who ended it!! I've moved on. You need to too."

But Travis didn't want to move on. He got up, started pacing, said he was going to see her, and got in a fight with his friends when they tried to stop him. One ended up calling his father for help.

When the friend's father showed up, he asked what was going on. "My son says you've been drinking a lot. You're fighting with your best friend."

"I just need to see Stacy," Travis said.

"I don't think this is about Stacy. I think it would be smart for you to see a professional. There are a lot of people who care about you. We're going to get you some help."

Travis realizes now that if his friends hadn't noticed and intervened, that day could have gone much differently. Only after they challenged him to get help did he begin to realize how unhealthy his behavior had been. His coping methods were harmful to him and those around him. His doctor prescribed an antidepressant to combat a chemical imbalance—a condition that had been going on much longer than his current circumstances suggested. Travis reconnected with his band, began exercising, and is living a much healthier life.

●

David, an executive with Elhart Automotive Campus who was trained in the **be nice.** action plan, received a call from one of his employees on Christmas Eve. While many families were having fun, eating good food, and enjoying time together, this employee, Joe, had just found out that his wife was leaving him. He went into a tailspin, went out and bought a lot of alcohol and started drinking it, and parked his truck in his garage that night while his wife and children were asleep inside. He closed the garage door and left the engine running.

But Joe, who had been trained in the **be nice.** program had the action plan in the back of his mind. He knew he needed help, and he reached out to someone he trusted. David convinced him to open the garage door, and they talked on the phone for the next thirty minutes until Joe was willing to agree that killing himself was not an option. Joe promised not to kill himself that night, and David promised to help him get professional counseling and support as soon as possible.

Joe, David, and Jeff worked together through the holidays to set Joe up with some appointments. They kept an eye on him at work and had frequent conversations. He is still seeing his counselor today, and things are going well. He is a very successful professional in his field and an integral part of the company.

Both Joe and David had worked with Wayne and been through the experience of dealing with his loss. And, as we've seen, being close to someone who has killed himself can increase the risk of taking one's own life. Joe knew that, and it took a lot of self-awareness to reach out the way he did. Fortunately, his cry for help saved his life.

Sometime later, Joe administered the action plan with one of his employees, a young man who had fallen into drug use and started showing up late for work. At first, Joe didn't realize the depth of this young man's need; he released him from employment because of his irresponsible behavior. But when Joe heard that this employee's parents had taken him to the hospital the next day for being at risk of suicide, he realized there was more to the story. After spending a couple of weeks in behavioral health treatment and taking some time to recover, Joe hired him back and has continued to work with him as he goes through counseling. He's doing very well today.

●

A middle school girl whose family was familiar with **be nice.** texted her mother frantically one day to say she had received a text from her former boyfriend. His text stated how hard the breakup was for him and that he didn't want to live anymore. The boy had been posting lyrics from a song about suicide, in which the artist had killed himself, and said it captured his life.

After texting her mother, the girl forwarded this boy's text to a social worker at the middle school and said she was very uncomfortable with it and worried about her classmate. Even before this mother could finish typing an email to the principal, the social worker called to let her know she had already contacted the student's mother.

Within minutes, everyone who needed to be involved was on top of the situation. And the principal told the girl who alerted everyone to the situation, "Thank you for noticing!"

She knew she had to report his text because she was trained in the **be nice.** action plan and was taught to take every threat seriously. She noticed the concerning text, invited herself to take it seriously, challenged herself to tell a trusted adult, and through her actions the boy received the attention he needed. They knew how to **be nice.**

●

A mother, father, and their young adult son "Nick" spent a weekend enjoying their time together during the Christmas holiday. It became obvious to the parents during that weekend that their son was not himself. This family has a history with mental illness and members of the family who manage mental illness, so they've equipped themselves with the **be nice.** action plan, as well as information from Saddleback Church Pastor Rick Warren's "Daily Hope," which talks about depression in relation to fear and anger. Confident in their knowledge, they made it their goal to find out what was going on with Nick.

After noticing several of their son's changes of behavior, they sat down to talk with him. He had dealt with depression for much of his life, so they approached him with a loving and caring conversation.

"We know you struggle with depression, and in the past you were dealing with feelings of fear and anger. Are you struggling with either of these today?"

"Anger, I guess."

"Okay, of all the things you're angry about, what are you most angry about the most today?"

"I'm just so overwhelmed. I don't have money to spend on Christmas this year. I don't aspire to be my own boss someday, even though I'm doing what I went to school for. I'm getting married, and I'm worried about being able to support my wife financially."

"So, it sounds like you're really dealing with anger and fear, right?" his parents asked.

"Yeah, I guess that's right," he answered.

The conversation then addressed whether their son's fears were well founded or not. They broke them down fear by fear. "First, you said you're worried about the ability to buy Christmas gifts. Christmas isn't about the gifts people receive but more about what you can give of yourself. Can you think of varied things that others would like to have from you for Christmas?"

"Yes, I suppose I can," he said. "I could make some things that I do at work for my family."

"That's a great idea!" So the parents went on to the next thing that their son had mentioned: "What makes you angry about your work?"

"I guess I'm a little overwhelmed and being too critical of myself because of all the other things that are on my mind."

"Well, that's certainly natural," the parents responded by pointing out what was good and right in their son's life. "Keep in mind that you're a very successful young man. You did well in school, learning your trade, and now you're applying it well. We're very proud of you."

Sensing a little relief in their son, they then went to the last subject on his mind—his upcoming wedding. "You mentioned that you were concerned about your ability to support your wife. Have you put together a budget for the wedding?"

"Yes, I have. It looks like with the help of you and her parents we'll have what we need for the wedding."

"That's great. You've shown responsibility in saving for your future. That isn't easy. You should be very proud of that."

"Well, I guess I may have been too hard on myself."

Though they felt good about the conversation, the parents still felt something gnawing at them. Given their son's battle with depression from Posttraumatic Stress Disorder (PTSD), they wanted to make sure he was okay and free from suicidal ideation, which he had experienced in earlier years. So, they challenged themselves to ask the question.

"You know we love you, right? We've seen these changes in your behavior, and we've had a great conversation about them. You've been very honest and open with us, but knowing of your depression and the experiences you've had, are you thinking of killing yourself?"

"No," he answered confidently, "and I thank you for asking."

The parents answered, "We love you and will continue to ask you this question when we are concerned. Our lives would never be the same without you."

●

Nick's experience is a great example of how this can work in a family situation, but not all families are comfortable talking about issues like

these. Many avoid these subjects as a matter of pride, shame, perceived communication barriers, or deeply ingrained family culture.
Due to circumstantial family history, confronting mental illness can be
difficult.

Some families' history creates a set of expectations, whether in-
tentionally or unintentionally, for the younger generation to live up to.
These standards may include the expectations for children to satisfy
their family by meeting certain guideposts, such as graduating from a
certain college, marrying a partner that meets the expectations of the
family, lifestyle choices, career choices, and others. Some people may
especially feel the pressure of living up to siblings' success and other
families' visible accomplishments. This creates a fear of not measuring
up. Sometimes all of these expectations create undue pressure on a
person who is trying to be successful in their own mind yet may feel like
a bit of a failure if they cannot satisfy these family expectations.

"Caleb" and his family are a prime example. Caleb's family is
very involved and well-liked in the community. Some people might
say they "have it all together." He knows he is loved by his family. But
Caleb feels that his family doesn't understand the pain he struggles
with, which makes it very lonely for him.

That presents a problem for Caleb, who has struggled with depression and anxiety since he was about ten. Because of his family's
perceptions about people who need help with such things, he was
always afraid to talk about it.

Caleb's friends noticed that his behavior had recently changed,
and one friend invited himself to have a conversation with him. During
the conversation, Caleb confessed a desire to kill himself, and his friend

didn't know what to do. Knowing that one of the dads, Mr. Denvir, felt comfortable talking about suicide, it made the most sense to reach out to him to help. Caleb agreed to talk with Mr. Denvir.

"I'm concerned about you, and your friends are concerned too," he told Caleb. "What's going on?"

Caleb was hesitant to open up at first, but after a little prodding, the emotions that he was holding back came spilling out. "I hate my life. I'm pissed off at myself all the time because I fall short of expectations—my family's expectations. My father expects a lot from me. So does my grandfather. I don't know how I can live up to what they want."

"It sounds like you're dealing with a lot. How are you dealing with this? Have you talked to anybody about this?" Mr. Denvir asked.

"Yes, off and on I've seen a counselor."

Mr. Denvir asked if Caleb was seeing a counselor now, to which he replied that he wasn't. Putting together the pieces that Caleb had been struggling with his emotions, that his friends had noticed, that he was no longer in counseling, and that he had expressed feelings of hopelessness, Mr. Denvir felt confident enough to further the conversation.

"Caleb, you just told me you hate your life, and you can't live up to expectations. I need to ask you, are you thinking of taking your life today?"

"I have thought about it, but not today," Caleb replied.

"Okay, we need to get you some help." Mr. Denvir and Caleb agreed to call a local access center together. The counseling center did an intake evaluation over the phone, and an appointment was scheduled for that week. Mr. Denvir followed up with Caleb after that conversation and has continued to be a constant support in his life.

The story of Caleb isn't over yet. He's doing pretty well, but he still struggles with the issues behind his depression, anxiety, and suicidal ideation. Not all of these conversations end with a perfect resolution and everything on the right track. You'll find that to be the case when you implement this action plan too. Knowing that people's lives are open-ended, it's important to always be noticing changes. That means, of course, that the "noticing" step in this plan never really ends and is always recycling. The other steps are just as vital. Every time you implement this plan, you are providing a compassionate service.

●

"Andi's" story began five years ago in Chicago, where she was living alone due to a new job. She noticed that her sleep had progressively became worse and found herself worrying more often. She was stressed emotionally and financially. Andi reached out to her mom and let her know that she wasn't doing well and was getting frustrated with her poor sleeping habits. Her mom invited herself to make the trip for a visit.

After the weekend was over, her mother could tell that Andi was not herself and thought she could be depressed. She did not have any experience with mental illness, but she invited herself to share her honest thoughts. Andi had never even considered herself to be associated with that word, and it scared her. Questions like *Why me?* and *How can I just snap out of this?* ran through her mind.

Andi took her mom's suggestion seriously, and she tried to manage her depression on her own for the next few weeks, but things got worse. As time went on, she was unable to maintain her job. She cried when she woke up, thinking about the day ahead, and still wasn't sleeping. Days would go by without her leaving her apartment.

Andi ignored every text from friends, who began to worry about her. She felt like she had hit rock bottom and had no idea what her next move was. Her story took a turn for the better with one simple decision.

Andi decided that she wanted to go along with her friends on a weekend getaway in Wisconsin. Andi had known about this trip for months, but since she had been ignoring her friends, they assumed she wasn't going. On a whim, she called up a friend whom she asked to pick her up when she drove through the city. Surprised and simply excited to finally hear from her, the friend said yes.

It was awkward and a challenge for Andi to face her friends and admit that she was not okay, but they made her feel welcomed. They were glad she was vulnerable and honest with them because they had been really worried about her. One of her buddies talked about how much she loved her job in Michigan and encouraged her to apply since they were hiring. For the first time in months, Andi felt a glimmer of hope and had an idea to chase.

A few months later, Andi was headed back to Michigan for the job and was looking forward to moving closer to her mom. Things had gradually improved since that weekend in Wisconsin, and she had a little pep in her step.

In the moment, she considered herself to be extremely lucky to have seemingly turned a corner with regards to her mental health. She was on the mend—or so she thought. What she didn't realize was that without any professional help for treating her depression, her journey was not over.

After five weeks at her new job, Andi's behavior changed again. She loved her new role and found herself engrossed with work. She would wake up at four o'clock and drive an hour to the gym, work until seven or nine o'clock at night, get home for a very late dinner, and go straight to bed.

Andi wondered, *Could this be sustainable?* She felt incredible. She was spending money she didn't have and even bought a new car. She was very active on social media, and her friends and acquaintances had noticed a major shift in her mood over time. To them, Andi appeared to be thriving. Little did she realize, another life-altering trip was on the horizon.

Andi planned a trip to Colorado with her mom and sister. On the morning she was supposed to leave, everything felt hectic and her thinking was erratic. She wasn't packed and had lost her flight information. Her mom was nervous she wasn't going to make it on time, especially since Andi's behavior in the weeks leading up to the trip were already causing her concern.

Upon landing in Colorado, Andi broke down to her mom and sister. Despite feeling on top of the world, she knew something was wrong and couldn't figure out what it was. Her sister was studying psychology at the time, and after piecing Andi's symptoms together, she had an idea as to what she was experiencing. They canceled the rest of the trip and flew home the next day. When she woke up from the car ride after the airport, they were at the University of Michigan Hospital, where she saw a doctor in the psychiatric emergency room.

Andi was diagnosed with bipolar disorder and spent nine days in the hospital. She said the doctors, nurses, assistants, and everyone in between made her feel comfortable and confident in the process. They laid out a plan for her, and she began taking medication. Now Andi knows that managing her mental health is an ongoing process. She attends therapy when needed and is on a consistent medication regimen.

Andi knows she has been through many ups and downs, and today she's doing fantastic. She didn't know the action plan when she was experiencing a change in her mental health, but she wants to make sure that other people are equipped with this tool. She volunteers her time as an advocate for the MHF and leans heavily on her support system of family and friends who empower her. And she's happy to share her story to decrease stigma and empower others to find a treatment option that works for them. She says not every day is great, but the good outweighs the bad by a long shot.

●

"Jasmine" noticed signs of depression in herself in high school, but she had many protective factors in place—sports, family, friends, volunteering—to help get her through. It wasn't until she went to college for the first time and being away from family for so long that it really started to affect her daily life.

Jasmine wanted to go home every weekend of her first college semester because she felt sad being away. She would isolate herself in her dorm room. Eventually, through her classes and roommates, she was able to find a group of friends who helped her focus on the good.

The friends decided to join a sorority, and it was one that often encouraged open and honest conversations about mental health. They shared a lot of great coping skills that Jasmine was able to use for her anxiety and that allowed her to have a very strong support system she could always lean on.

But halfway through her junior year, she had feelings of hopelessness and sadness when her best friend died in a car accident. Jasmine began isolating herself from her friends. They often reached out, but she ignored them. She found herself simply going through the motions of daily life, and slowly her depression took control.

Jasmine's roommates noticed symptoms of her depression but realized she needed more support. They even invited themselves to reach out to Jasmine's family and friends from home and encouraged her to make an appointment at the counseling center. When Jasmine was unable to make it for herself, because of her depression and anxiety, the friends scheduled an appointment for her. They gave her hope that she could enjoy life again.

Through trial and error, Jasmine was able to find a counselor who worked for her. They talked honestly about her feelings of anxiety, stress, and depression and helped her find medication and healthy habits that worked. Her friends continue to check in on her.

●

These are just a few real stories of real people with real struggles with mental illness. When we realize that 80 percent of us can be a "lifeguard" for someone who is struggling with depression or anxiety, and that there is a simple four-step action plan to help those in need, healthier families and communities will be the result when we put it into action.

More Than an Action Plan

Remember that the action plan we have outlined and explained in the last five chapters is one piece of mental health awareness and suicide prevention. It's part of a larger whole—a culture of being "nice" that incorporates each of the n, i, c, and e elements into everyday life. Think about what that might look like upstream, outside of this conversation when intervention is needed:

- If we are *noticing* all the time, we respect other people and what is good and right about each one. We look for things to value in people, find ways to honor and affirm them, and treat everyone with a welcoming attitude.

- If we are *inviting* ourselves into conversations and inviting others to respond to them, we will reach out to our family members, friends, neighbors, and coworkers to see how they are doing. When someone loses a job, or if we see someone sitting alone all the time, we go over and ask how they are. When someone goes through a breakup, we check in to see what's going on (without giving the impression that we're trying to pry). We live out our interest in others.

- If we are **challenging** people, we ask the hard questions when we need to and confront the stigma of mental illness by being willing to talk about it as a common aspect of life that everyone needs to be aware of. We don't tiptoe around important issues, and we don't confront in an aggressive or accusatory way. We simply have the conversations we need to have out of concern for people.

- If we are **empowering** others, we always let them know where to get appropriate help with whatever they are facing and offer to walk with them through the steps they need to take, even before they get into a crisis situation. People need to have an understanding of their protective factors—access to and utilizing services, surrounding themselves with supportive individuals, involvement in activities outside of work and school, faith and spirituality, and keeping strong morals. In addition, what is good for our physical health is also key to our mental health—nutrition, sleep, limiting drugs and alcohol, meditation, positive self-talk, and exercise.

And that's what the big picture is all about—heading off crisis situations before they even come up. The action plan we've discussed is a great tool for those kinds of situations, and it's absolutely essential when someone's life might be on the line. But earlier prevention is even better. Everyone ideally wants to live in a warm and welcoming environment. We can all do our part in creating one.

So pay attention to people's mental health. Understand what mental health is, and make yourself aware of the signs, symptoms, and risk factors that could be a mental health concern. Make sure people know there are resources for them, no matter what they are going through. And, when a crisis situation seems to arise, jump in "downstream" with the **be nice.** action plan as soon as it's needed.

Changing the Culture
with be nice.

Written by Jeff Elhart and Christy Buck

Emotions come to the surface easily when people have spent time together relaxing and unwinding. There's nothing unusual about that. But when several coworkers got up to leave after an evening of food, drink, and conversation, one remained in his seat and began to cry.

Fortunately, the business where this group of friends worked had offered training in the **be nice.** program, and some of these coworkers had been through it. One of them asked the emotion-stricken man what was going on and learned that his life was falling apart—his wife had been having an affair, he was on the verge of divorce, and he was wrestling with some pretty huge issues in other areas of his life. He had been carrying enormous burdens, and no one knew about them. Then the question was asked: "Are you thinking about killing yourself?" The man could not answer with a clear "no." Within minutes, some of these coworkers were driving their friend to a place to get help.

That's an example of how the action plan can work in the course of community life, but it doesn't happen if people haven't been educated in it, and education doesn't happen if a community and its organizations have not been proactive in their approach to this problem. By definition, prevention is not reactive. It is the result of people anticipating and preparing for a potential issue. Stephen Covey identified being proactive as the first of his famous Seven Habits of Highly Effective People because it empowers us not to be victims of our circumstances but to shape them. Proactive people focus on things they can do something about and take the initiative to address them. If depression is one of the most treatable diseases and suicide one of the most preventable deaths, we cannot afford only to wait for crisis events to happen and then react to them. If we want to be effective at suicide prevention, we will have to be proactive in getting the right tools into our communities.

We've discussed how our society needs a tool to help people with mental illness and potentially save them from suicide, much as we have "stop, drop, and roll" to rescue people from a fire. We have always had people who are concerned about this problem, and we have always had long-term approaches like counseling and medical treatments that can help over time. But because of the subtleties of mental illness and the stigma associated with it, we have not viewed it as we view fire prevention and safety. We have not given society as a whole any sort of intervention plan that can be utilized quickly, efficiently, and up-front in a crisis situation.

That's what **be nice.** is all about. Businesses wouldn't be success-ful for very long if they took the same approach that we often take with social issues. If a customer takes his or her car in to a repair shop and says it won't run, the business has to do more than diagnose the problem. "Your engine is shot, but we don't have the expertise or the personnel to fix it" is not a helpful response. Why would people take their cars to mechanics if they could simply talk about the problem without offering solutions?

Society has only begun becoming comfortable with talking about mental illness, depression, and suicide in the last fifty years, and then really only in the last couple of decades with any depth. Mental health organizations have worked tirelessly to increase that trend. Recent events like high-profile suicides and school shootings have brought the issues even more to the surface. But if there are no solutions to go along with the discussion, we can talk about these things all day long without getting anywhere. Nothing will happen. With the rise of these tragic events, we are now at a point where we absolutely have to do more than talk about the problem. We have to have a solution, a tool like "stop, drop, and roll" that anyone can use.

be nice. is a tool similar to "stop, drop, and roll." Like "stop, drop, and roll," it is relatively easy to implement *if* people understand its importance and are willing to be proactive. It can fit into society's toolbox to equip friends, neighbors, relatives, coworkers, fellow church members, acquaintances, strangers—in other words, *anyone*—to be prepared to notice potentially critical situations. We want a society full of "lifeguards" who are well-trained in preventative care.

This is everyone's job, a social responsibility. We are called to "love our neighbor." We know how to do that when we see someone who is visibly, physically disabled because it doesn't take much expertise to help someone across the street. But seeing someone who is mentally struggling and knowing how to help is a far more difficult issue. **be nice.** can make it much easier.

Our society craves action-oriented responses. When we recognize a problem, we want it fixed. If there's a rise in suicides among students, we look for solutions. But often we look for a quick fix without having the right tools. To visualize this, work from the bottom of this funnel:

The base of the triangle is knowledge. You have to know what the signs and risk factors of a mental illness are and how to approach them. With that knowledge comes confidence—the belief that your knowledge is accurate and your approach is appropriate. Then comes action at the top of the triangle, the visible steps a person takes to address the concern. Our society very often discusses action and makes plans without having the base of knowledge or the confidence that our knowledge can be used appropriately and effectively.

Knowledge breeds confidence. Confidence breeds action. The knowledge we learn in this book facilitates upstream understanding of the big picture of mental illness and suicide prevention. This knowledge is important to have as a foundation so we can use it to move downstream in order to have an immediate impact on how people think, act, and feel . . . and potentially participate in saving someone's life.

In the aftermath of the Parkland, Florida, tragedy in 2018, students, teachers, administrators, and parents discussed action steps with our government leaders at a White House session hosted by the president, vice president, and secretary of education. Among the many issues they discussed was the topic of mental illness. One of the participants was Darrell Scott, whose daughter Rachel was killed in the Columbine school massacre, and he emphasized one simple principle: "We must create a culture of connectedness. We must create a culture in which our classmates become our friends." That's a powerful statement— the awareness that almost all school shootings have come at the hands of young men who were disconnected and happened in the context of depression or mental illness.

Mental illness, particularly depression, is expected to be one of the major health burdens of the coming decades, affecting schools, businesses, and other organizations. Considering that depression is one of the main causes of chronic illness in the developed world, it stands to reason that we need to equip both children and adults to manage and treat it—to recognize it in themselves and others, and to know what steps to take to get help. This needs to be an open discussion that produces knowledge, then confidence, and then appropriate tools to take action.

This is where the **be nice.** action plan provides fuel for the race to educate our youth and adults about mental illness awareness and suicide prevention. We have been involved in getting it into the communities of western Michigan for several years, and it is growing beyond our region into other parts of the U.S. and the world. Community members have donated financial resources to support the program, and numerous classes have been taught in businesses, places of worship, retirement communities, veterans associations, youth organizations, and schools. It is creating a common language and a culture of connection, and it is saving lives.

Entryways into the Community

With the high frequency of mental illness—one in five will experience it at some point in their lives—and the fact that roughly half of those affected will never receive treatment, awareness and prevention efforts become a community issue.[25] We need widespread understanding of mental health and widespread opportunities and avenues for getting help. The more people who understand and are equipped to notice, invite, challenge, and empower, the more other people will receive the treatment they need and the healthier our communities will become.

We have found that segmenting the community is a good way to start. Society is organized into groups, and each of these groups has

---

[25] National Alliance on Mental Illness (NAMI).

its own cultural dynamics. By segmenting, we can find appropriate entryways into schools, businesses, places of worship, special interest groups, charitable organizations, associations of veterans or retirees or professionals, and so on. The possibilities are numerous. Organizations that are created specifically to help others—women in transition, people in hardship situations, etc.—are especially open to receiving instruction and training to equip their people for suicide prevention. The three types of organizations we have worked with most extensively so far are schools, businesses, and places of worship.

The densest segment of the population is also the segment most affected by depression. About 75 percent of all mental illness is diagnosed before the age of twenty-four, but fewer than 50 percent of all people affected are ever professionally treated for it.[26] That tells us how vitally important it is to implement the **be nice.** program in schools.

The teenage years have always been a confusing time, but life is more confusing for young people growing up now than it was for those growing up fifty years ago. Students face an abundance of choices, not all of them healthy; they are growing up in a highly competitive job market; they are under pressure to make lifelong decisions earlier than ever; and they are bombarded by an overwhelming number of stimuli and sources of information that strain even the most mature brains. Mental health concerns begin early in many lives, and sometimes they can be a matter of life and death. Government programs have committed to addressing the problem by training teachers to identify at-risk students, which is certainly helpful, but an even more

---

[26] National Alliance on Mental Illness (NAMI).

effective approach is to give fellow students an understanding of the issues. An approach like **be nice.** does more than address problems one on one; it removes the stigma, opens discussion, and increases awareness for an entire generation. It encourages a culture of connection among a peer group in which disconnections often begin.

The dynamics are not quite the same in businesses and faith institutions, but the training can have similar effects. Middle-aged men are another high-risk group, and often they suffer from depression without the people around them picking up on the signs or knowing how to help if they do. By taking **be nice.** into businesses, faith institutions, and other community organizations, thousands are being equipped to intervene in situations like the one that began this chapter—a person at risk for suicide receiving help from people who know how to notice, invite, challenge, and empower.

Overcoming Obstacles

An environment that normalizes noticing, inviting, challenging, and empowering does not come simply through a textbook or even a training session. It comes from a culture change, and every school, business, or organization has its unique culture that provides both an opportunity and a set of obstacles for addressing mental health issues and suicide prevention.

As we've seen, those obstacles may include the stigma associated with mental illness. They also include some administrative challenges, decision-makers and administrators who already have a lot on their plate, leaders of organizations not having a background in psychology or counseling, and the financial costs of implementing a program. The obstacles are easier to overcome when the needs are prominent—for example, in the aftermath of a tragedy that heightens awareness—but it's less work in the long run to focus on prevention, that "upstream" culture change discussed earlier. Educating the community in issues related to mental health and suicide is one of the best things we can do to create a healthier society. Integrating **be nice.** into a community's organizations, such as businesses, schools, and places of worship, is an effective way to do that.

No obstacle is insurmountable. Each kind of organization—in fact, each individual organization—has its own pathway into a program for mental health awareness and suicide prevention that makes sense to that organization and its culture. For some, like faith communities, it may begin with prayer. Jeff serves on the executive committee for a unique public-private sector coalition in Washington, DC, called the National Action Alliance for Suicide Prevention. Its goal is to reduce suicide by 20 percent by 2025. One segment of society they work with is the faith community, and efforts to bring the National Day of Prayer for Faith, Hope, and Life to faith communities across the nation in support of World Suicide Prevention Day (September 10), which helps promote the work of faith-based organizations in instilling hope, facilitating social connections, and helping people understand mental health challenges. By simply praying for members who are facing depression, anxiety, bipolar disorder, schizophrenia, and problems with alcohol and other substances, even without mentioning their names, we send a message that these members are just as important and deserving of care and support as those with physical challenges. Many people in crisis seek the support of their faith communities and leaders, and for many of them prayer is a meaningful response that demonstrates love and compassion.

Advocacy is another pathway toward implementation. Communities need champions for the cause, people who will take it upon themselves to approach businesses, schools, and other organizations. Advocates and champions can make the job of decision-makers easier by promoting, planning, initiating, and organizing programs in ways that fit the culture of the organization and promote positive change. Christy and the MHF staff serve on several local, regional, and statewide coalitions, using **be nice.** as a main catalyst for change.

Changing the Culture

When education and awareness initiatives are implemented at an organization-wide level, lives change. Schools and businesses are reporting back to the MHF with story after story of how perceptions have changed and people are getting needed help.

In one school where we led a few workshops, a student group wanted to launch the **be nice.** program by organizing an assembly and issuing a challenge to the student body. A lot of work goes into planning something like that, and in the process, the organizing team wanted to identify within its own group anyone who had ever struggled with a mental illness or had contemplated suicide. The morning of the assembly, one of the students came forward to say he had contemplated suicide a week earlier, and he wanted to share his story. We talked through the concerns with him to make sure he realized the repercussions—the responses he might get, the possibility of both positive and negative attention, etc.—and he decided to go through with it. Not only did students respond overwhelmingly positively to his story, but it became a catalyst for other students coming forward to talk comfortably about their own struggles and thoughts. That assembly took place five years ago, and recently this young man reached out to let us know what a difference the program made in his life as he continued through college and now into adulthood. It is impossible to know if any lives were saved the day he shared his story, but from the stories students told, the impact of one student's courageous act was significant. We do know that putting **be nice.** into action helped struggling students get the support they needed.

A similar launch at another school hit a setback the night before the assembly was to occur. One of the most popular students at the school tweeted his contempt for the event—"Just another waste of time for bully prevention," he said (although in harsher and more colorful terms). The student leadership team began to panic, worried they would just embarrass themselves at an event that was being portrayed as stupid and nobody wanted to attend. But they had worked hard on preparing for this event, felt strongly about how important its message was, and moved forward with it in spite of their fears. As the assembly began, they saw their vocal critic sitting front and center facing the stage. They proceeded with their presentation, describing the notice, invite, challenge, and empower principles, and making sure they issued a challenge to the rest of the student body at the end to sign a banner signifying whether they were on board or not. The critic didn't sign it—then. But he did get back on Twitter to say the program was much more impactful than he had imagined and that he would sign the banner the next day. The momentum encouraged other students to open up about their struggles and work to change the culture of the school.

The stories from businesses look a little different, but they can have just as much impact. A multinational engineering firm with sixteen hundred employees launched **be nice.** to one of its plants by teaching the four principles of notice, invite, challenge, and empower over the course of four shift meetings. With leadership teams initiating the program, they built activities around each letter of *nice* and soon saw an increase in the number of participants in their Employee Assistance Program, as well as a more positive corporate culture overall. A global furniture company with eight thousand employees took a somewhat different approach, beginning with an overview of **be nice.** for employees, and then giving employees the opportunity to participate in a more intensive eight-hour Mental Health First Aid course. This company, too, has seen positive results.

Once trained in the action plan, people apply their knowledge in other areas of life beyond the schools, businesses, or organizations where they were trained. We've heard stories of elementary school students encouraging their classmates who are going through difficult experiences—abusive backgrounds, bullying, loneliness, foster care—by using **be nice.** principles. We've heard from law enforcement agencies about officers and administrators advocating for the program in their children's schools and finding ways to take the time to talk and listen to people they encounter in their work. The story that began this chapter involved a group of coworkers, but they walked through the **be nice.** steps in a way that demonstrated they could do it with anyone in any setting. Parents have picked up on the principles from their children who have gone through the program. In other words, changing the culture within a school, business, place of worship, or government agency has the potential to change the culture of the community as a whole. Noticing, inviting, challenging, and empowering shouldn't be contained within an organization. They are tools to carry into every area of life.

These stories are anecdotal evidence, but they point to much larger numbers. Research has demonstrated that these stories are multiplied again and again and make a real difference. When students see Post-it notes over the school walls that point out all the great things about them and their peers; when students report changes in behavior to school counselors and employees report them to their supervisors out of genuine concern; when a negative environment transforms into a positive, affirming one, the importance of mental health awareness and suicide prevention becomes clear. The **be nice.** action plan is a concrete way to respond to the tragic headlines we see and a simple tool to use in our daily lives in the way we connect with other people every day.

chapter

13

Saving Lives
with be nice.

Written by Jeff Elhart and Christy Buck

Over the course of this book, a lot of information has been presented that demonstrates the overwhelming needs in our society for mental health awareness and suicide prevention. We've told stories that put human faces on these needs and demonstrated how they can be addressed. We've offered a simple but powerful tool that anyone can use to make a significant difference in the lives of those around them. And we've suggested a number of ways for this tool to be implemented in personal lives, families, schools, workplaces, and communities.

This is a lot of information to absorb, and much of it can feel very heavy. So take a few moments to set the specifics aside and envision the opportunities we have. Use your imagination. What might increased levels of mental health awareness and effective suicide prevention lead to in our world?

- Imagine a society in which anyone struggling with unhealthy thoughts, emotions, and behaviors can easily find the help they need and feel no embarrassment in doing so.

- Imagine a family, school, or work environment in which each person is protective of and compassionate toward others' mental and emotional well-being.

- Imagine living in a world in which human interaction is characterized by mutual respect, affirmation, acceptance, and encouragement, even when disagreements and conflict occur.

- Imagine spending every day at work, school, or home knowing that you will be valued as a human being there—and being intentional about valuing others too.

Society would be much healthier than the one we often experience, wouldn't it? Most people would agree that these are desirable scenarios. The bigger question is whether this kind of society is possible.

The answer to that question depends on you. It depends on many other people too, but it begins with each person making a decision to help create the kind of environment they want to live in. Every one of us can be part of the solution to the needs we've been discussing throughout this book.

The good news is that most people agree. A 2020 survey, taken in early months of the COVID-19 pandemic, suggests that more than 80 percent say it's more important than ever to make suicide prevention a national priority. About 95 percent of American adults believe suicide can be prevented and would be ready to take action if they thought someone close to them was considering it. Yet two-thirds of them recognized that there are barriers to taking action, including not knowing what to say, not having enough knowledge about the issues, and not feeling comfortable with the topic.[27] In other words, an overwhelming majority of people want to do more, but most aren't sure what that would be.

That's where **be nice.** fills an enormous need in our society. It raises awareness, recognizes that many people need more understanding and a tool for implementation, and makes practical knowledge easily used. But this program and good intentions aren't enough. Change most often occurs when people proactively take steps to make it happen.

The Importance of Being Proactive

Stephen Covey defines proactivity as more than just taking an initiative.[28] He focuses on "response-ability"—the ability and freedom to choose our response. There's a difference between reactive thinking, in which a stimulus causes an immediate response, and proactivity, which allows space between the stimulus and response for a real choice to be made.

Covey says that proactive people focus their efforts on the things they can do something about: health, children, problems at work, and anything else in their circle of influence. Reactive people focus on things over which they have little control: the national debt, terrorism,

---

[27] Harris Poll on behalf of the National Action Alliance for Suicide Prevention (Action Alliance), the American Foundation for Suicide Prevention (AFSP), the Suicide Prevention Resource Center (SPRC), and Education Development Center (EDC), February 2020.

[28] Stephen R. Covey, *The 7 Habits of Highly Effective People: Powerful Lessons in Personal Change* (New York: Simon & Schuster, 1989).

the weather, and so on. It's important to be aware of where we're spending our energies if we're going to be proactive people. We have a choice in our communities to be proactive. We can move from being victims of situations like suicide to being empowered to address them. How we react to the horrible results of a death by suicide is the difference between embracing the root causes and letting the things we can't control take over. We actually have some control over mental illness and suicide. As we've emphasized throughout this book, mental illness is one of the most treatable diseases, and suicide is one of the most preventable deaths.

Preventing suicide involves everyone in the community, both at an individual level and at the level of government, public health, health care, employers, education, faith institutions, the media, and community organizations. It requires the efforts of as many people as possible from as many situations as possible.

Education is a key. One of the purposes of this book is to inform and educate proactively. Far too often, organizations or individuals react and then seek education as a result of a tragic event, which is understandable when unavoidable. However, we have means for equipping ourselves with the tools of prevention. We already know that one in five of us in the U.S. will suffer from mental illness, which means the four in five who will not suffer from these illnesses can make a profound difference by becoming educated with the warning signs and how to address them.

Many in the western Michigan community have taken up that challenge, and we believe many more across the country and the world are rising up to do the same. At a recent gathering of various individuals and organizations using **be nice.** to raise awareness and equip people to be proactive, nearly all found the simplicity of the program to be a major asset for their students, parents, employees, congregants, and other interested parties. They commented on how user-friendly they have found it to be. Many people who have been exposed to the action plan have remarked, in surprise, that they no longer feel alone on these issues of awareness and prevention. And most agreed that providing this education was "good business" in their community, whether for schools, places of worship, businesses, or families. They understood that we cannot afford to wait for others to take the lead. The time to join the effort is now.

Communities can offer programs and events to increase a sense of belonging among residents. Teaching coping and problem-solving skills helps people manage challenges with their relationships, jobs, health, or other concerns. That can happen in a number of ways.

Schools can teach students the skills to manage challenges of relationships and school stressors. Much of the Mental Health Foundation's work is directed toward sustaining their school program that helps students, parents, and teachers recognize the symptoms of depression and the warning signs of suicide in themselves, friends, or family members. Its educational program also encourages students to set aside stereotypes and treat fellow classmates with understanding, compassion, and acceptance. The **be nice.** curriculum is also designed to help young people who may be personally affected by mental illness to get past the stigma and seek treatment. Research shows that this approach has been remarkably successful in transforming the culture in schools into more accepting and affirming environments.

Churches and other faith communities can provide a safe place for people to be encouraged to seek help and offer assistance to those in need, which naturally fits their mission and goals as places of refuge, support, and social transformation.

Employers can apply policies that create a healthy environment and reduce stigma related to seeking help for a mental health concern, which is beneficial for a business, at both a personal level and in bottom-line results. A positive workplace culture leads to numerous benefits for individual employees and the workplace as a whole. Mentally healthy employees are happier, more energetic, more motivated, and more productive employees. Employers can create that environment by promoting employee health and well-being, supporting at-risk employees, and having plans in place to respond to people showing warning signs of a crisis. They can encourage employees to seek help and provide referrals to mental health, substance use disorder, legal, or financial counseling services as needed.

Media outlets can provide resources when covering topics such as mental health and suicide and avoid using headlines or including details that increase or trigger a person who is at risk. Evidence suggests that media stories of people positively coping in suicidal moments helps prevent suicide.[29]

We've seen **be nice.** recast in the form of a sermon series in a Christian church setting, events for schoolteachers, student-led school assemblies reaching all grade levels, training seminars, and much more. High school students have gathered together to share their best practices for implementing the program. College students have come

---

[29] National Institute of Mental Health (NIMH).

together to encourage each other to notice what is good and right about their fellow students and embrace the different personalities, interests, and backgrounds among them. Faith leaders have made efforts to dispel the "sinful" connotations of suicide and mental illness and to raise awareness of the health concerns involved. Business leaders have found creative ways to alert their people to warning signs and address them proactively—and increased their business efficiency and productivity as a pleasant side effect.

What Are You Going to Do?

We saw earlier in this chapter that a majority of Americans have a strong desire to be proactive with mental illness and suicide prevention but are insecure about knowing how to address these issues. At the very least, there seems to be an overwhelming movement to recognize one of the most prevalent diseases in our country. The greatest area of need has been education. Perhaps that's why many of those leading the way right now are high school and college students—people regularly very close to education.

The MHF has been a significant part of community efforts to make the **be nice.** program available to schools, faith communities, businesses, and other interested parties through training events and other public presentations. Thousands of community members have become familiar with the action plan and are implementing it in their areas of work and home life. It is changing the culture community by community, organization by organization, family by family, and person by person.

In the last chapter, we looked at some of the ways that communities, businesses, schools, faith organizations, and families are doing this, but let's bring it down to a more personal level. Ask yourself a very important question: *What are you going to do in response to what we've learned?* If you've continued reading this book this far, you likely understand that suicide rates are a problem that needs to be addressed, and you may agree that it will take a society-wide approach. Probably, you've also seen some opportunities in these pages—open doors for community involvement, personal conversations, approaches to take in your family or at your workplace, and more. So what are you going to do?

There are many ways you could answer that question. First, look for the exercise at the end of this book that will challenge you to put to work your **be nice.** knowledge and confidence in the action plan. This will help you assemble a mental health safety plan for your family. The thirty minutes invested will give you a roadmap of identifying any opportunities to help improve or potentially save a life.

Another action step is to review the basics of each **be nice.** action plan step on benice.org. This is a four-part video series, with each video covering one of the four action steps of **be nice.** followed by a ten-question quiz to test your knowledge. Share this site with your family, friends, coworkers, and others.

And on a grander scale, you can develop a plan to carry out this education to your respective community. Over the past five years, nearly 500,000 K-12 students and 2,000 adults have experienced the impact of this lifesaving tool in West Michigan thanks to the generous support of our community. This was accomplished by (1) initiating three community donor-advised funds and (2) helping form two others raising almost $2 million in just four years. These funds enable the MHF to serve five West Michigan counties with a population of about one million. They are used to provide matching funds to schools and faith communities that commit to the **be nice.** education tool on mental illness awareness and suicide prevention. It is well on its way to changing the way people think about and respond to mental illness, depression, and potential suicide and creating one common language for this field of concern in the community.

Most of all, resolve to make a difference. Plan some steps that move you in that direction. Envision families, schools, workplaces, and communities that are healthier because of your presence and involvement in them. Put what you've learned into action to help save lives.

chapter
14

Managing Your
Mental Health

Written by Jeff Elhart and Christy Buck

Our mental health is with us every day, and some days are more challenging than others. You don't have to identify with having a mental
illness to nurture your mental health. Here are some practical tools
you can invite yourself to do in order to practice good mental health.
These are not magic formulas, but they do help, sometimes quite dramatically.

Notice the Good and Right

Practice optimistic thinking. This is not just telling yourself to be happy;
it is about building resilience within yourself. Negative thoughts can
seem natural and inevitable to someone who is depressed or anxious,
but you actually have a choice about what you think. You may have
difficulty believing this at first, and optimism may feel like a real chal-

lenge. Deeply ingrained thought patterns are difficult to redirect, but they really can change. Practice hopeful ones. Make them a habit. Your innermost being also responds to the sound of your voice, so speak plenty of positive words to yourself. (These words may feel forced and artificial at first, but that's because they go against negative thoughts that you have long believed are true. Your heart will catch up to your words eventually.) When you do this, keep reminding yourself that you aren't trying to convince yourself of something that isn't true. You're convincing yourself of what is true, which your thought patterns have obscured and distorted over time. This takes practice, patience, and persistence. But the more you think and speak positively and optimistically, the more your outlook begins to change.

This is not an unrealistic idealism. You don't have to ignore real stresses and problems to be an optimist. You simply need to believe that you have the power to create opportunities for good things to happen. There is no reason to assume your prospects are bleak and ample reason to believe they are good. Your future is very likely to include a lot of good things in it. And when you believe this, it becomes a self-fulling prophecy to a degree. Optimists are far less likely to suffer from major illnesses, more likely to develop healthy habits and healthy relationships, and more likely to live longer.[30] So several times a day, choose to think and speak positively and optimistically about yourself, your circumstances, and the people around you. Even if this goes against the grain of your old thoughts, the grain will eventually begin to turn.

---

[30] Ciro Converano et al., "Optimism and Its Impact on Mental and Physical Well-Being," *Clinical Practice and Epidemiology in Mental Health* 6 (2010): 25–29, https://benthamopen.com/FULLTEXT/CPEMH-6-25.

Invite Yourself

Practice gratitude. Grateful people experience many of the same health and emotional benefits that optimists do.[31] And everyone has some things to be grateful for. Start small if you need to, but just start. Count your blessings. Keep a journal of good experiences, memories, relationships, and possibilities in your life. Write down any positive experience, no matter how small. Don't let yourself be overwhelmed by the future or feel regrets from the past. Stay in the moment. A few minutes of gratitude several times a day can do wonders for your outlook.

Challenge Yourself to Step Outside Your Comfort Zone

Volunteer. It is scientifically proven that giving—putting the well-being of others before ourselves—creates positive, satisfying feelings.[32] As with the practice of optimism and gratitude, selfless works positively affect brain chemistry. They stimulate the brain's reward centers and produce an emotional high that has lasting effects. This makes sense, doesn't it? One of the pitfalls of depression and anxiety is a tendency to turn inward, focus on problems, and magnify them. Turning outward undoes those negative effects. Volunteering reduces stress, increases cognitive function, and has positive physical effects.

---

[31] Amy Morin, "7 Scientifically Proven Benefits of Gratitude," Psychology Today, April 3, 2015, www.psychologytoday.com/us/blog/what-mentally-strong-people-dont-do/201504/7-scientifically-proven-benefits-gratitude.

[32] "Helping People, Changing Lives: The 6 Health Benefits of Volunteering," Mayo Clinic, May 18, 2017, www.mayoclinichealthsystem.org/hometown-health/speaking-of-health/helping-people-changing-lives-the-6-health-benefits-of-volunteering.

Empower Yourself

Strengthen social connections. Strong relationships make us feel more connected to family and friends, and we are happier and healthier as a result; this is a protective factor. Even a modest strengthening of relationships can have these positive effects. Many people struggling with depression feel alone and isolated, sometimes because of insecurities about themselves or underdeveloped social skills that make them fear rejection or feel awkward or unloved. These perceptions are almost always exaggerated, and a little effort to reach out and connect with someone is a great place to start. Deep, committed relationships can be wonderful, but that's not the goal here. A few quality relationships can reduce our sense of aloneness significantly.

Live with purpose. Depression and anxiety are intensified by purposelessness, and the best way to reverse that trend is to find purpose in something bigger than one's self. This can be a religious faith, a social cause, a problem to solve, a passion to cultivate—anything that takes the focus off your immediate circumstances and puts it on a meaningful goal. Human beings seem wired to live and work for something larger than themselves, and when that sense of purpose disappears or gets distorted, depression sets in.[33]

If You Think You Might Be Depressed

In addition to the above steps, there are several things you can do to specifically address depression. And if you aren't sure, there are self-assessments you can take online that will help you know if you

---

[33] Rick Warren's *The Purpose Driven Life* is a great resource to get started with this.

really are struggling with this very common problem. You can receive a quick online self-assessment at www.benice.org/get-help/mental-health-screening-tool.

The relationship between body and mind is strong and substantial, so many treatments for depression will include physical activities. In particular, getting enough (but not too much) sleep, getting regular exercise, getting out into sunlight, and eating a healthy diet (avoiding over-indulgence in sugar, alcohol, and other depressive substances) are extremely helpful changes to make. In fact, many counselors and therapists say that physical exercise is an even more powerful treatment than antidepressant medications. It's a great place to begin—not as a substitute for medication, if it is needed, but as an additional way to address mood disorders. The challenge is that one of the effects of depression is low energy, which means that you most need exercise at a time when you least feel like doing it. This will take some initiative and willpower, but it's worth it. In addition, drink plenty of water, develop consistent routines in your sleep habits, and be patient with yourself. Changes take time.

There are things you can do to reorient your inner life too. As mentioned above in the suggestions to practice optimism, gratitude, and some kind of service to others, a shift of focus can be invaluable in combatting depression. Even if you naturally tend to look inward, make a consistent effort to look outward and upward. Faith and love—meaningful attitudes and acts of selflessness—are powerful in expanding perspectives, enriching life, and creating positive feelings. These are simple approaches, but they aren't simplistic. You can probably find myriad ways of adapting this shift of focus to your personality and interests. But however you implement them, they are very effective in combatting depressing thought patterns.

If You Struggle with Anxiety

Anxiety can put enormous stress on our minds and bodies. In its basic form, it's a necessary response to real threats. We are designed to feel anxious about some things, at least momentarily. It comes from a fight-or-flight response that is helpful and lifesaving in many situations. But nearly one out of five people has an anxiety disorder, which means for many, anxiety is triggered by non-threatening thoughts or events and lasts much longer than it should. And for many, it can impair cognitive ability and their ability to function in everyday activities. It can be paralyzing and create extremely distressing thoughts.

These approaches can help if you struggle with anxiety:

- *Ask yourself the right questions.* You'll need to train yourself to do this, but asking some very objective questions whenever you feel anxious can deescalate your feelings. For example, *Is this anxious thought accurate or exaggerated? Is the danger real or imagined? Am I overreacting?* Separating false alarms from the real ones can help you manage this condition.

- *Work backwards.* Most of us try to combat anxious thoughts within our own minds. That can be helpful (see the point above), but combatting it at the level of its physical symptoms can be very effective too. When we're anxious, our blood pressure and heartbeat increase, and we breathe faster. So try managing those responses by breathing more slowly and deeply for a few minutes. (This is why people often say, "Take a deep breath," in a stressful situation. It's nature's way to counteract anxiety's symptoms.) Close your eyes and imagine more peaceful situations. Acting calmly doesn't always produce calm, but sometimes it can. The mind very often responds to physical cues.

- *Change your environment.* Environmental cues have a profound effect on our thoughts, and sometimes getting away from those associated with our anxiety works wonders. If you're in an anxiety-inducing situation, step out of the room if you can. Don't avoid all your stressors—if your bills are causing anxiety, you still need to pay them; if a difficult conversation is necessary, avoiding it will probably just magnify the problem—but take a break and take in the bigger picture. Go for a walk. (Exercise reduces anxiety just as it helps with depression.) Look out the window and notice something beautiful about the world around you. Shift your focus onto something much more peaceful.

- *Calm your mind.* Meditation and prayer can reduce anxiety and bring a sense of peace. We talked about changing your outward environment in the point above; these calming activities change your inner environment.

Don't Wait to Get Help . . .

The suggestions above can be very helpful. So can therapy. Millions of people have found relief from struggles with anxiety and depression by seeking the help of a professional trained to diagnose and treat these illnesses. There is no shame in doing so, and it can be lifechanging. You will have an opportunity to explore in more depth the thoughts, feelings, and behaviors you've been experiencing, to understand some of the sources behind them, and to discover positive coping skills and protective factors that will empower you to embrace a healthier life. Whatever you are feeling, you are not in it alone. Many have walked this road before you and come out on the other side. There are qualified people who are ready and able to help you. Rid yourself the additional burden of trying to deal with this alone.

Remember what you just learned in this book—**be nice**. and save a life. It may just be your own.

Excercises,
Appendices,
Epilogues, &
Acknowledgments

Exercises

Putting be nice. into Action for Your Family

Now that you've finished reading the body of this book, you've gained confidence through understanding more of how people think, act, and feel. Let's apply some potentially lifesaving action based on that knowledge.

Following are summaries of each chapter in the format of the **be nice.** funnel: Knowledge breeds confidence, and confidence breeds action. By investing just thirty minutes in reviewing this section, answering the questions, and committing to the challenges posed, you will have a game plan to help improve and potentially save lives in your family.

Chapters 1 & 2: Could I Have Prevented My Brother's Suicide?

Knowledge—After reading these chapters, I realize that suicide is not a selfish act. It is an action taken by someone who is sick with a mental illness. Their pain exceeds their ability to cope with feelings of helplessness, hopelessness, and worthlessness.

Confidence—I am confident that I can make the effort to notice warning signs in those around me for depression and suicidal ideation.

Action—I will communicate with my family members about any noticeable changes in their lives by inviting myself to have a loving and caring conversation. I will also plan on having a mental health checkup for myself and my family at least once a year with our prima-ry care physicians.

Chapter 3: Understanding Mental Illness and Suicide

Knowledge—One in five people struggle with a mental illness in our country. The most common disability in the world is anxiety, followed by depression. Less than 50 percent of adults suffering with these dis-eases will receive professional help.

Confidence—To determine how mental illness may impact my family, I first identify how many people are in my family:

_____ Number of people in my immediate family who reside in my home (include husband, wife, children, anyone else in the home)

Plus _____ Number of parents who live outside my home

Plus _____ Number of grandparents who live outside my home

Plus _____ Number of aunts and uncles who live outside my home

Plus _____ Number of first cousins who live outside my home

*Equals _____ Total number of immediate family and extended family members

Multiply by 20% or 0.20, which equals the national average of people with a mental health disorder

**Equals _____ Total number of potential family members with mental illness

Action—This is the number of members in my family who, according to national statistics, may be struggling with a mental illness today. I can have an impact on how they think, act, and feel by learning and using the tools in this book.

Chapter 4: Nobody Is Immune

Knowledge—Anyone can be affected by mental illness. The densest segment of people who die by suicide is males aged thirty-five to fifty-four years. It is the second leading cause of death in ten- to thirty-four-year-olds. Twenty percent of suicides are sixty-five and older.

Confidence—With the knowledge I've gained in this chapter, I know that I can make an impact. The fact that anyone in my family can fit the demographics of suicide victims makes me want to know potentially how to save lives.

Action—Mental illnesses need to be brought to the forefront of awareness. I can do this by finding events and resources in my community that bring awareness to mental health and suicide prevention. Therefore, now that I know how to notice, invite, challenge, and empower, I am confident of taking action to help people who are struggling with depression and/or suicidal thoughts.

Chapter 5: Dispelling the Myths

Knowledge—I know now that if I ask someone whether they are thinking of killing themselves, this question does *not* put the idea in their head. Rather, this question can help.

Confidence—True or false: I am confident that this question is exactly what most people need to hear from a loved one or someone who cares.

Action—It's important to continue to learn about mental health and suicide prevention to protect myself and the people around me. I can make the **be nice.** action plan a part of my daily life. I can take it a step further by bringing the **be nice.** program into my school, workplace, or community environment.

Chapter 6: A Program and an Action Plan

Knowledge—The **be nice.** action plan, which is more than a simple call to kindness, gives me the tools to take action when it comes to mental health among myself and those around me.

Confidence—Since I now know that mental illness, especially depression, can be a silent disease, I have more confidence to invite myself into someone's life knowing I can have a positive impact on how they think, act, and feel.

Action—I will meditate or pray for the next five minutes concerning who in my life may be in need of this simple action plan. I will take action to notice, invite, challenge, and empower.

Chapter 7: notice

Knowledge—I will recognize what is right about anyone. I will also notice what is different. If someone exhibits changes in their behavior lasting two weeks or longer, I'm going to invite myself to ask the person, "Are you okay?"

Confidence—I better know how anyone in my family or circle of friends, coworkers, or acquaintances has exhibited a visible change in their behavior in the last few weeks.

Action—By recognizing what makes someone special, I will acknowledge this in person or in writing.

Chapter 8: invite

Knowledge—When I invite myself to have a loving and caring conversation with someone who may be struggling with depression, that person will appreciate my reaching out. This person may be in pain and may not know how to reach out or get help as this book provides it.

Confidence—The more I invite myself to talk openly about mental health and the more someone who is struggling feels more comfortable with me, the more confident I become to take action.

Action—I am going to invite myself to have a loving and caring conversation with the person that I have identified. I am going to say, "I've noticed that you typically have a positive outlook, but lately you don't seem like yourself. I've noticed you haven't been enjoying the things you typically love to do. I'm concerned about you and genuinely care. Are you feeling okay?"

Chapter 9: challenge

Knowledge—I know that mental illness can be a silent disease, and 90 percent of the people who die by suicide currently struggle with a mental illness, mostly depression. I know that by asking, "Are you thinking of killing yourself?" I can open the door to a potentially lifesaving conversation.

Confidence—Even if I don't feel confident in asking this important question, I do feel confident that I can find a trusted adult or professional who will. Stigma is the number one reason people do not speak up when they are struggling. I can decrease stigma by facilitating conversations about mental health, illness, and treatment.

Action—If a person I've identified has exhibited signs of suicide, I will initiate a loving and caring conversation about what I've noticed. "I am worried about you, and I need to ask you a question. Are you thinking of killing yourself?" To help prepare myself to ask this tough question, I might practice saying it out loud to gain more confidence.

Chapter 10: empower

Knowledge—People who suffer with mental illness may need immediate professional attention, especially if they have been experiencing changes in their behavior lasting two weeks or longer. Those with suicidal ideation need immediate attention. I know there are coping skills and protective factors I can implement into own my life to build resiliency and protect my mental health. I also know what resources are available when it comes to mental health.

Confidence—I realize that my friend, relative, or coworker suffering with a mental illness might need confidence to seek professional help or treatment on their own; I can empower them with resources and offer to accompany them through the process.

Action—When I've developed a relationship of trust with someone who has exhibited numerous changes in their day-to-day behavior, it is my responsibility to help that person get professional help. This does not mean merely advising them to go the hospital on their own, I will act and take them myself.

Chapter 11: be nice. in Action

Knowledge—The **be nice.** action plan has proven to be an effective way to notice risk factors that people face regarding depression and suicidal ideation. This plan gives me the tools to take action.

    Confidence—The **be nice.** action plan is not complicated. Most situations connected with depression are not complicated. Unfortunately, there is too much commentary out there that depicts depression and suicide as very complex, steering many of us away from our friends, relatives, coworkers, and acquaintances because we are afraid of saying or doing the wrong thing.

    Action—I will make it my mission to create real-life success stories by simply noticing, inviting, challenging, and empowering. Period. I believe I can have a positive impact on _____'s life now by using the **be nice.** action plan.

Chapter 12: Changing the Culture with be nice.

Knowledge—I know that depression does not discriminate. I also know that 20 percent of people in our country struggle with a mental illness.

    Confidence—Every community is impacted with mental illness, and I am very likely to come into contact with someone who is struggling in my school, workplace, faith institution, neighborhood, voting district, veteran association, book club, golf group, workout group, and city or town, and I can be a catalyst for change and empowerment.

Action—I can initiate change. I will initiate mental illness aware-ness and suicide prevention education in my areas of influence. One way I will do this is by spreading knowledge about the **be nice.** action plan along with things I've learned in this book.

Chapter 13: Saving Lives with be nice.

Knowledge—I know there are many ways that I and the people around me can take action to protect our mental health before a concern becomes an illness and requires professional help. Protective factors and coping skills such as exercise, social connection, volunteering, and generally being an active person can make a big difference in our overall health.

Confidence—I am confident I can be a source of encouragement and engagement with my peers to get them involved in protective factors.

Action—I will take it upon myself to be an accountability partner to someone by involving them in an activity that both of us enjoy.

Chapter 14: Managing Your Mental Health

Knowledge—If symptoms last two weeks or longer, I know that be-cause mental illness is a disease, like diabetes or a heart condition, it is treatable.

Confidence—I am convinced that the pain of mental illness is real, but hope is real too. Managing a mental illness is not a weakness.

I have the tools to address this illness, and if treatment's needed, that's okay.

Action—If I am in a crisis situation, I will take the knowledge I have learned from this book and plan to take the following action steps immediately:

1. I will contact a family member, school counselor, pastor, or friend to let them know that I am considering suicide.

2. I will call the National Suicide Hotline at 1-800-273-8255 with my friend/family member to inquire for professional help, or . . .

3. I will ask my friend or family member to take me to the hospital emergency room for a professional assessment of my condition.

4. I will not follow through with any plans to kill myself.

5. I will allow my friend or family member to be my accountability partner until I receive the professional help I deserve.

An Epilogue

Written by Christy Buck

I was twelve, the youngest of three girls, when my father died. My mother went from the typical PTA leader mom, who cooked a big Greek dinner every night and always had time to laugh and play with her daughters, to a businesswoman. I assumed then that she was doing well. I assume now that she grieved while she worked. After all, she had three daughters to nurture through their losses. Perhaps I didn't want to recognize that her smiles were more forced and less frequent.

Three years later, while we four were vacationing in Florida, my mother's smile vanished. She stayed in the room for several days, and by the time we'd driven back to Michigan, she was catatonic, though I didn't know it then. My oldest sister took her to a local institution, where she was hospitalized for three weeks.

By the time I was sixteen, my sisters were grown and gone. My mother and I lived alone. Though she still worked sometimes, often there were days she refused to get out of bed.

Throughout my teens, I never really understood. I never had a name for what was wrong with my mother. Only once was I able to voice my deepest fear—when, during another episode, the days in bed stretched into weeks, and I told my best girlfriend that I was afraid that my mom was going to kill herself while I was at school. I drove her back to the institution and signed commitment papers that night, and still, I didn't really know what was going on.

While I studied for my recreational therapy degree, I read about depression in textbooks and never made the connection. I took an internship with a mental health facility and never made the connection. It wasn't until I conceived of a clubhouse for people with mental illness during my first job that it finally hit me: my mother had gone through a series of life's greatest stresses in a period of just a few years. She was depressed. She broke down the first time because she had never been treated for depression. She broke down again and again because stigma kept treatment and help a secret.

My job as executive director of the Mental Health Foundation of West Michigan is to fulfill its mission "to equip individuals with the knowledge to recognize, understand, accept, and take action when it comes to mental health." I bring my whole heart to the job, in part because it puts me in just the right place to carry out my own life's mission: to educate people about mental illness; to remove stigma so that more people can really understand what may be happening in their own lives; and to help people identify the signs of depression or other mental illness and know where to go and how to help themselves or others who struggle with depression, ultimately preventing suicide.

Originally called Live, Laugh, Love, today's Mental Health Foundation has supported my dream to develop and deliver programs about mental health and suicide prevention. I am grateful to have a board that supports the vision for the MHF to be the best source to improve and save lives through proactive mental health and suicide prevention education. I have grand visions and hopes that **be nice.** will be a national model of changing, saving, and improving lives in every school district, business, faith institution, and community in the U.S.

An Epilogue

Written by Jeff Elhart

You may be curious to know how a mother can weather the storm of losing her son to depression by suicide. The road has been rugged. Let me have her tell you for herself . . . after I tell you a quick story of Mom's endurance.

You may recall reading in chapter 12 about the Mental Health Foundation of West Michigan having been invited to engage a school in northern Michigan in the **be nice**. education program and action plan. That high school lost a boy to suicide in October 2015, just six months after Wayne's death, it happened in my mother's hometown. Hearing this news and still raw from Wayne's death, my mom wanted to take action to help her community and local school. She wanted to bring the **be nice**. program and action plan to this small village, which has approximately 270 K-12 students. Her goal was to raise money and present the gift of this program to the school superintendent the day of the young man's funeral. She asked me how much that would cost. I frankly had no idea at the time, so I threw out a number that I was certain would cover the cost.

"When is the funeral?" I asked Mom.

"Tomorrow!" she said.

"Sounds like you have twenty-four hours to raise some money, Mom! You can do it!"

For the next several hours, I received phone calls with updates on her progress. The next day, my eighty-six-year-old mother had raised $11,500! This was the beginning of the Wayne Elhart **be nice**. Memorial

Funds, which are donor-advised funds at three Michigan community foundations: Oceana County, Holland/Zeeland, and Muskegon. Her actions were the impetus for creating these donor-advised funds. As a result, I have been able to champion the mission of providing matching funds to schools, faith institutions, businesses, and other organizations who commit to the **be nice.** education program. The funds total nearly $2 million as of this writing. Had it not been for the generous support of the communities that these funds serve, over 700,000 youth and adults would not have been equipped with the **be nice.** education program. And probably, neither would this book.

Thank you, Mom. I love you.

• • •

Now in her words . . .

It's been six years since Wayne died. I just turned ninety years old as this book is being printed. Wayne would be turning sixty-seven this year. God, I miss him. I think about him every day. I miss him every single day. I speak to him every day.

From my journal, September 7, 2015 (five and a half months after Wayne died):

Hi Wayne, just checking in on you. You won't believe what happened today. I saw a monarch that reminded me of you. There you were. Checking on me. You inspired me to write these words in a form of a poem that will remind me that every time I see a monarch I will know it is you, Wayne.

A Butterfly Message

A monarch butterfly I saw today,
His wings were damp.
I let him cling to my finger,
Till his wings were dry.
I know he was trying hard to fly away,
Where he was going,
I do not know.
But I do know the butterfly was here,
To let me know,
That my son Wayne is OK.
I said, "I love you and miss you."
And watched him fly away.
Where I do not know,
But I sent him on his way,
To land near someone else,
Who is missing a loved one,
And say it's OK.

I felt so much better because the monarch was your message to me, and that's why I decided I would write you a note every day. I'm going to have this poem typed and put on the refrigerator so you will remind me when I have a low day to get up and move, laugh, and have fun because you don't want me to grieve. It's very hard, Wayne, but I know you wouldn't want that.

I'm going to finish this now and write more tomorrow.

I'm tired and thank you and God for visiting me today. I know you will come again.

Love you and miss you,

Mom

APPENDIX A

be nice. Testimonials

The following are comments from several people who have experienced the **be nice.** program in a business environment—not necessarily as recipients of someone's implementing the action plan but as those who have benefitted from its overall effects and have a very positive impression of how the program has changed the culture they work in.

1. "I see now that I must focus on the things that matter—my relationships, my work, and my family. If I do my part to make these things better, I believe that life will in time become easier to bear. Who'd have thought so? It is time for me to start caring again—time for the real me to return. I now look forward to the future and see possibility rather than darkness."

2. "I think we stop and ask ourselves what the person we are working with may be going through and how our words help or hurt that person. We work more as a family and try to think of each other's feelings—that we must be observant of any changes in a person we might see. Sometimes how we are acting speaks volumes about what is going on in our personal lives. . . . I try to notice how my fellow employees and customers are acting. I try to read my fellow employees' body language and listen to what they are saying or not saying. I let our customers share

their stories. I want to be a good listener because sometimes that is what people need. Sometimes I have even used **be nice.** with customers. I have noticed them and invited them to step into relationship with me or someone I think they might relate to. Next I have challenged them to take a step to becoming and feeling better as a person. Then I try to empower them and let them know I will be there or find someone to be there for them, but that they are truly in charge of their lives."

3. "**be nice.** has provided us with the confidence, self-awareness, and climate of caring for others. It has given us 'permission' to cross department lines by noticing what is right with others so we may notice when something changes, and then feeling secure in inviting ourselves to have a conversation. . . . I am a mother of two girls. The need for **be nice.** has come up in their personal lives with peers and family members who have struggled. I have found it to be an essential tool for life!"

4. "**be nice.** has had an immense and positive impact on the culture and environment here. The goal is to erase the stigma of mental health so we can talk openly about any issues and have a safe and non-judgmental place to openly share and ask for help. Another byproduct of having **be nice.** on campus is that it brings coworkers closer together, which promotes better teamwork and a healthier place to work. It puts everyone on a level playing field when it comes to mental health and suicide prevention awareness."

5. "Prior to **be nice.**, mental health awareness and suicide prevention were never openly talked about. To be able to sit

down with my children and talk about things without its feeling weird is a great feeling. I have taken many phone calls, text messages, and emails outside of work from employees and non-employees. If nothing else, sometimes signs need to be recognized that there may be a potential problem or someone at risk, and we just need to get them headed in the right direction and to the proper people who can help."

6. "I feel more than just an employee at a company and merely someone on the payroll. It has allowed me to become more open, made me feel comfortable sharing things that maybe in the past I wouldn't have, and brought me extreme joy and a sense of accomplishment when we all come together in a time of need—whether for me personally or another teammate who may be struggling. . . . I feel much better equipped to deal with and understand mental health issues and how it may affect people."

7. "Prior to learning the **be nice.** action plan, I had no clue of what to look for. . . . I am not quite sure what I would've done if someone had told me they were struggling mentally or were thinking about suicide. It was taboo. You weren't supposed to talk about it. I often think back many years and wonder how many times I could've applied **be nice.** to people had I been aware of and educated about mental health and suicide prevention. I imagine I would have used it a lot, especially in my teen and early adulthood years."

APPENDIX B

How to Deal with How You Feel (Three Questions to Manage Your Emotions)

The following, by Rick Warren, is a tool I (Jeff) have found very valuable in helping to identify the "what" of a person's depression. By identifying specifically what mentally strains a person, the **be nice.** action plan can be enhanced with the probable explanation that the person experiences human emotions of fear (worry) and/or anger (guilt). These two common emotions have a significant impact on how we think, act, and feel. While Rick addresses this to Christians, the principles can be helpful to anyone regardless of religious background.

---

by Rick Warren

The Bible says in 1 Peter 4:2, "From now on, then, you must live the rest of your earthly lives controlled by God's will and not by human desires" (TEV).

What are human desires? Your emotions and affections. Now that you are a Christ-follower, your life should be controlled by God's will, not by how you feel.

Let me give you three questions to ask about your emotions when you're trying to figure out how to deal with how you feel. When you're angry or upset or frustrated—whatever you're feeling—ask these three questions:

1. *"What's the real reason I'm feeling this?"* Maybe the answer is fear or worry. Maybe it relates to something your dad said to you years ago, and when your husband said it to you, he got all the anger against your dad that you pent up.

2. *"Is it true?"* Is what you're feeling at that moment true? There's a point in the Bible where Elijah gets so discouraged that he went to God and complained, "God, I'm the only one in the entire nation of Israel left serving you." And God challenged him, saying, "Are you kidding me? I've got all these people who are still serving me! You're acting like you're the only one trying to do the right thing in the whole world! No. That's not true."

3. *"Is what I'm feeling helping me or hurting me?"* Will you get what you want by continuing to feel this way? A lot of feelings we have feel natural, but they're actually self-defeating.

Let's say you go to a restaurant, and the service is extremely slow. You wait a long time to be served, and then a couple comes in 15 minutes after you and gets their meal before you do. You get increasingly more irritated until you feel something welling up inside you.

What's the real reason you're feeling that way? You're hungry!

Is it true? Yes. You're frustrated because the service is slow. But is your emotion helping or hurting? Do you get better service by getting angry at the server? Absolutely not.

Does nagging work? Has it ever worked? When some-
body tells you all the things you're doing wrong, does it make
you want to change? No! All it does is make you defensive.

When you ask yourself these three questions, you get a
better grip on why you feel the way you do and what you
need to do to help the situation.

That's called managing your emotions.[34]

Pastor Warren continues sharing in his video sermon series on this message that we need to identify what emotion we're experiencing. He
challenges his readers and viewers to recall, "I can't tame it until I
name it. I can't solve a problem until I identify it."

What triggered the emotion? If the person can't talk about it, the
emotion may already be out of control and may very well take it out
on their body. "When you swallow your emotion your stomach keeps
score," Rick says. "Emotions were not meant to be swallowed; they
were meant to be shared."

How will you use your own emotions? Will you swallow them where
they will continue to eat you alive from the inside out? Or will you be
vulnerable and share them with a friend for the good of helping others
as God wants us to? Don't waste a pain. Use it for good. Channel it if
you're not going to change it.

---

[34] Reprinted with kind permission of Rick Warren.

APPENDIX C

Glossary of Mental Illness and Suicide Terms

People experience different types of mental illnesses or disorders, and they can often occur at the same time. They can occur over a short period of time or be episodic. This means that the mental illness comes and goes with discrete beginnings and ends. Mental illness can also be ongoing or long-lasting. There are more than two hundred classified types of mental illness. Some of the main types of mental illness and disorders are listed below; however, this list is not exhaustive.

Anxiety Disorders

People with anxiety disorders respond to certain objects or situations with fear and dread or terror. Anxiety disorders include generalized anxiety disorder, social anxiety, panic disorders, and phobias.

Attention-Deficit/Hyperactivity Disorder

Attention-deficit/hyperactivity disorder (ADHD) is one of the most common childhood mental disorders. It can continue through adolescence and adulthood. People diagnosed with ADHD may have trouble paying attention, controlling impulsive behaviors (may act without thinking about what the result will be), or be overly active.

Disruptive Behavioral Disorders

Behavioral disorders involve a pattern of disruptive behaviors in children that last for at least six months and cause problems in school, at home, and in social situations. Behavioral symptoms can also continue into adulthood.

Depression and Other Mood Disorders

While bad moods are common and usually pass in a short period, people suffering from mood disorders live with more constant and severe symptoms. People living with this mental illness find that their mood impacts both mental and psychological well-being, nearly every day, and often for much of the day.

It is estimated that one in ten adults suffer from some type of mood disorder, with the most common conditions being depression and bipolar disorder. With proper diagnosis and treatment, most of those living with mood disorders lead healthy, normal, and productive lives. If left untreated, this illness can affect role functioning, quality of life, and many long-lasting physical health problems such as diabetes and heart disease.

Eating Disorders

Eating disorders involve obsessive and sometimes distressing thoughts and behaviors, including:

- Reduction of food intake
- Overeating

- Feelings of depression or distress
- Concern about weight, body shape, poor self-image

Common types of eating disorders include anorexia, bulimia, and binge eating.

Personality Disorders

People with personality disorders have extreme and inflexible personality traits that cause problems in work, school, or social relationships. These disorders include antisocial and borderline personality disorder.

Posttraumatic Stress Disorder (PTSD)

A person can get PTSD after living through or seeing a traumatic event, such as war, a hurricane, physical abuse, or a serious accident. This mental illness disorder can also result from very personal attacks from others in the form of sexual abuse and domestic violence. PTSD can make someone feel stressed and afraid after the danger is over. People with PTSD may experience symptoms like reliving the event over and over, sleep problems, becoming very upset if something causes memories of the event, constantly looking for possible threats, and emotional changes like irritability, outbursts, helplessness, or feelings of numbness.

Schizophrenia Spectrum and Other Psychotic Disorders

People with psychotic disorders hear, see, and believe things that aren't real or true. They may also show signs of disorganized thinking, confused speech, and muddled or abnormal motor behavior. An example of a psychotic disorder is schizophrenia. People with schizophrenia may also have low motivation and blunted emotions.

Substance Use Disorders

Substance use disorders occur when frequent or repeated use of alcohol and/or drugs causes significant impairment, such as health problems, disability, and failure to meet major responsibilities at work, school, or home. Substance use problems can be fatal to the user or others. Examples include drunk driving fatalities and drug overdoses. Mental illnesses and substance use disorders often occur together. Sometimes one disorder can be a contributing factor to or can make the other worse. Sometimes they simply occur at the same time.

Suicide

Suicide is death caused by injuring oneself with the intent to die. A suicide attempt is when someone harms themself with any intent to end their life, but they do not die as a result of their actions.

Many factors can increase the risk for suicide or protect against it. Suicide is connected to other forms of injury and violence. For example, people who have experienced violence, including child abuse, bullying, or sexual violence have a higher suicide risk.

Being connected to family and community support and having easy access to health care can decrease suicidal thoughts and behaviors.[35]

---

[35] "Suicide Prevention," Centers for Disease Control and Prevention, March 23, 2021, www.cdc.gov/suicide/facts/.

APPENDIX D

If You Are Feeling Suicidal Right Now . . .

If you are feeling suicidal now, please stop long enough to read this. It will only take about five minutes. I do not want to talk you out of your bad feelings. I am not a therapist or other mental health profession-al—only someone who knows what it is like to be in pain.

I don't know who you are, or why you are reading this page. I only know that for the moment, you're reading it, and that is good. I can assume that you are here because you are troubled and considering ending your life. If it were possible, I would prefer to be there with you at this moment, to sit with you and talk, face to face and heart to heart. But since that is not possible, we will have to make do with this.

I have known a lot of people who have wanted to kill themselves, so I have some small idea of what you might be feeling. I know that you might not be up to reading a long book, so I am going to keep this short. While we are together here for the next five minutes, I have five simple, practical things I would like to share with you. I won't argue with you about whether you should kill yourself. But I assume that if you are thinking about it, you feel pretty bad.

Well, you're still reading, and that's very good. I'd like to ask you to stay with me for the rest of this page. I hope it means that you're at least a tiny bit unsure, somewhere deep inside, about whether or not you really will end your life. Often people feel that, even in the deepest darkness of despair. Being unsure about dying is okay and normal. The fact that you are still alive at this minute means you are still a little bit unsure. It means that even while you want to die, at the same time some part of you still wants to live. So let's hang on to that and keep going for a few more minutes.

Start by considering this statement:

Suicide is not chosen; it happens when pain exceeds resources for coping with pain.

That's all it's about. You are not a bad person, or crazy, or weak, or flawed because you feel suicidal. It doesn't even mean that you really want to die. It only means that you have more pain than you can cope with right now. If I start piling weights on your shoulders, you will eventually collapse if I add enough weights . . . no matter how much you want to remain standing. Willpower has nothing to do with it. Of course you would cheer yourself up, if you could.

Don't accept it if someone tells you, "That's not enough to be suicidal about." There are many kinds of pain that may lead to suicide. Whether or not the pain is bearable may differ from person to person. What might be bearable to someone else may not be bearable to you. The point at which the pain becomes unbearable depends on what kinds of coping resources you have. Individuals vary greatly in their capacity to withstand pain.

When pain exceeds pain-coping resources, suicidal feelings are the result. Suicide is neither wrong nor right; it is not a defect of character; it is morally neutral. It is simply an imbalance of pain versus coping resources.

You can survive suicidal feelings if you do either of two things: (1)

find a way to reduce your pain, or (2) find a way to increase your coping resources. Both are possible.

Now I want to tell you five things to think about.

1. You need to hear that people do get through this—even people who feel as badly as you are feeling now. Statistically, there is a very good chance that you are going to live. I hope that this information gives you some sense of hope.

2. Give yourself some distance. Say to yourself, "I will wait twenty-four hours before I do anything." Or a week. Remember that feelings and actions are two different things—just because you feel like killing yourself doesn't mean that you have to actually do it right this minute. Put some distance between your suicidal feelings and suicidal action. Even if it's just twenty-four hours. You have already done it for five minutes, just by reading this page. You can do it for another five minutes by continuing to read this page. Keep going, and realize that while you still feel suicidal, you are not, at this moment, acting on it. That is very encouraging to me, and I hope it is to you.

3. People often turn to suicide because they are seeking relief from pain. Remember that relief is a feeling. And you have to be alive to feel it. You will not feel the relief you so desperately seek if you are dead.

4. Some people will react badly to your suicidal feelings, either because they are frightened, or angry; they may actually increase

your pain instead of helping you, despite their intentions, by saying or doing thoughtless things. You have to understand that
their bad reactions are about their fears, not about you.

But there are people out there who can be with you in this
horrible time, and will not judge you, or argue with you, or send
you to a hospital, or try to talk you out of how badly you feel.
They will simply care for you. Find one of them. Now. Use your
twenty-four hours, or your week, and tell someone what's going
on with you. It is okay to ask for help. Try this:

- Send an anonymous e-mail to The Samaritans (see
  www.samaritans.org for details)
- Call the National Suicide Prevention Lifeline at 1-800-
  273-8255 (TTY:1-800-799-4TTY)
- Text HOME to 741741
- Look in the front of your phone book for a crisis line
- Call a psychotherapist
- Carefully choose a friend or minister or rabbi, some-
  one who is likely to listen

But don't give yourself the additional burden of trying to deal
with this alone. Just talking about how you got to where you
are releases an awful lot of the pressure, and it might be just the
additional coping resource you need to regain your balance.

5.   Suicidal feelings are, in and of themselves, traumatic. After they
     subside, you need to continue caring for yourself. Therapy is a

really good idea. So are the various self-help groups available both in your community and on the Internet.

Well, it's been a few minutes and you're still with me. I'm really glad.

Since you have made it this far, you deserve a reward. I think you should reward yourself by giving yourself a gift. The gift you will give yourself is a coping resource. Remember, a couple of pages ago, I said that the idea is to make sure you have more coping resources than you have pain. So let's give you another coping resource—or two, or ten!—until they outnumber your sources of pain.

Now, while this may have given you some small relief, the best coping resource we can give you is another human being to talk with. If you find someone who wants to listen and tell them how you are feeling and how you got to this point, you will have increased your coping resources by one. Hopefully, the first person you choose won't be the last. There are a lot of people out there who really want to hear from you. It's time to start looking around for one of them.[36]

---

[36] Reprinted with permission. "Suicide: Read This First" (https://www.metanoia.org/suicide) was written by Martha Ainsworth based on work by David Conroy, Ph.D. To talk with a caring listener about your suicidal feelings, in the U.S. call 1-800-SUICIDE any time, day or night. Online, send an anonymous e-mail to jo@samaritans.org for confidential and non-judgmental help, or visit https://www.samaritans.org.

Acknowledgments

by Christy Buck

In a career that has spanned over thirty-four years, acknowledging all those who have provided an impact and to whom I am deeply grateful can be daunting. There are so many individuals who have come in and out of my life personally and professionally, and whether the interactions have been big or small, they have shaped who I am as a wife, mother, sister, *yiayia*, daughter, executive director, and community leader.

To past coworkers and members of Transitions Day Treatment and the 201 Club, where I started my career in the field of mental health in 1986: I learned that good treatment, supports, and having a safe place free of stigma and where one can feel a sense of purpose are essential to mental health recovery.

To Greg Dziadosz and Margaret Chappell for seeing in me the passion, skills, and dedication to lead the Mental Health Foundation and begin the journey of educating our community and reducing the stigma of mental health disorders.

To some of the amazing women in my life who have been examples of grace, compassion, dedication, fearlessness, and faith: my mother, Stella Tsilimigras; my amazing sisters Sophia Clark and Ellen Cokinos; my mentor, Liz Sarafis; mother-in-law, Kitty Buck (memories eternal); and Barb Davidson. My other sisters, Terri DeBoer and Jennifer Travis: you continue to offer support and inspiration to both my life and my career.

To the cocreators of our original education program, "Live, Laugh, Love" (now **be nice.** Extension), Leisa Bageris, Susan Meekhof, and Larissa Payton. The creation of this program opened the door for the MHF to educate young people in the basics of mental health and the warning signs of suicide.

To the superintendents, principals, and teachers who were bold and brave enough to bring mental health and suicide prevention education to their schools at a time when any conversation about suicide brought fear and apprehension, recognizing specifically friends at Grandville Public Schools: Ron Caniff, Teresa Waterbury, Chris Vander Slice (memory eternal) and Janelle Groya. From other districts: Sara Ahmicasaube, Vivian Marsiglia, and Todd Kamstra for pioneering in their respective districts.

These same individuals took the leap with us a second time around when we launched the **be nice.** program beyond having a one-and done assembly. We knew working mental health education and awareness into the school culture was key to preventing severe levels of mental illness and suicide. We have big dreams and expectations in all that we do, but we can't do it alone!

To my friends: my church community at Holy Trinity Greek Orthodox Church and Ionian Village, my Grandville neighbors, friends through my kids' sports, my kids' friends and their parents . . . always eager to be the connection between **be nice.** and communities. Those volunteering for parades, fundraising, sporting **be nice.** gear, serving on committees, or performing as an extra in a **be nice.** movie . . . the list goes on!

To all who have worked, interned, or volunteered at the Mental

Health Foundation, each and every one of you has had your hand in the work that continues to this day! Whether you were putting tattoos on kids at a Maranda Park Party, mailing thank you's after Stomp Out Stigma, or jurying art for Shining Through, you have made a difference and have been instrumental in churning the successes of the organization.

To those who have lost loved ones to suicide: you are the engine that gives me my momentum; your recounting stories of personal loss and healing fuels my drive to continue to change, improve, and save lives.

To Mental Health Foundation board members, past and present, always willing to keep the train going forward and keeping us on track, with special recognition to Jeff Elhart for acknowledging that **be nice.** can make a difference in lives and for allowing me to coauthor this book, a dedication to his brother, Wayne.

To Jeff's agent, Chip Brown, and Proper Media for helping to make this a reality and for finding us Chris Tiegreen to help put words onto paper. This project has formed new friendships!

To the staff of the Mental Health Foundation, the best of coworkers: Larissa Payton, my friend, my assistant, the emergency contact for my kids in elementary school, the longest on this journey! It's been amazing to see the reality that internships, an AmeriCorps placement, a grant-funded position, and volunteering can lead to careers for Kandice Sloop, Cat Lanting, Therran Hines, Isabella Buck, and Mary Aldrich. Lastly, those who saw and see the endless possibilities of **be nice.**: Jessica Jones and Jennifer Reynolds.

And ultimately, my family—my kids, Demetrios, Katerina, and Isabella—for their countless hours of volunteering, which is inherent in our Greek heritage and a vital part of our family values. (Basically, they didn't have a choice.) My daughter-in-law, Photini, and son-in-law, Mark, who just boarded this train have no idea what they are in for, but they look incredible in **be nice.** swag. My husband, Tim, who began this journey by my side as a coworker in 1987, who continues to ride the rails with me, sacrificing his time and supporting my spirit of continuing to seek innovative ways to empower our great community.

Acknowledgments

by Jeff Elhart

Love

To the love of my life. Thank you to Cherie Elhart, my wife of forty-one years and my best friend since we were just twelve years young. Without your undying love and support, this book would not have been possible. You have traveled this world with me all the way. While the path has not been without challenges, you have supported me as you promised you would in our vows. Thank you for your forgiveness, your patience, and your love. Wayne was the brother you never had. You made him smile—and laugh.

To the love from my family. My sons, Jake Elhart and Ben Elhart, and their loving wives, Danielle and Allison. Jake, you are still so much like your "ole Uncle Wayno"; Ben, you have experienced the pain that your Uncle Weenie lived, and I pray for Wayne's spirit to always fill you with perseverance.

To my parents for their unconditional love. To my dad, Ken Elhart: your love for your sons, Wayne and me, has always been known despite the trials that Wayne and I put you through. You have been the greatest father, mentor, and coach that a son could hope for. To my stepmother, Margaret Elhart: thank you for taking us kids in as your own. To my mother, Barbara Davidson: whether in the hospital or in the bathroom over tears about a breakup with my girlfriend Cherie in junior high school, you were always there for me. Mom, you have experienced the greatest loss as Wayne's mom, and yet you were the first to take action when you decided to canvas your small community for financial support to introduce **be nice.** into your local school (all within twenty-four hours)! To my stepfather, Gene Davidson: thank you for your support and especially your genuine, special friendship with Wayne through sailing, cigars, and Golden Cadillacs.

To my dear sister-in-law, Kathy. Thank you for your unselfish acts that have allowed me to take up this initiative to provide mental illness awareness and suicide prevention in your husband Wayne's honor. To my brother-in-law, Bruce, Wayne's first business partner just out of college, whose mid-'70s carpet cleaning business in Boulder, Colorado, was known by its slogan, "No carpet is too shaggy for us." And to my sister-in-law, Judie, who was lucky to find Bruce as her husband and somehow managed to clean up the messes left by him and Wayne.

Joy

I wish to sincerely thank several people who gave me joy during these years since Wayne's death and have always supported me in my drive to make a difference in Wayne's honor. They are Christie and David Eaton, cofounders of www.Speak2Save.org, whose mission is to empower people to speak up and prevent suicide. Thanks to your self-produced movie Hope Bridge, I am 80 percent rid of my guilt over Wayne's death. Thanks to Sara Lewakowski, executive director of Mosaic Counseling, who offers hope and healing for all by providing accessible and affordable professional counseling services (the most incredible delivery model of professional counseling that I have seen across the country).

Thank you to the Mental Health Foundation of West Michigan,

including the entire staff—especially (despite the risk of singling out some staff) Cat Lanting, Jessica Jones, and Larissa Payton. And most importantly to my great friend, coauthor, and adopted member of our family, Christy Buck. Christy, you have provided the answer to prayer. It is an honor to have a sister in this difficult but rewarding work. Thank you for the opportunity to connect with you just two months after Wayne's death and let the good Lord do his work through our work together.

Peace and Forbearance

To the team at Elhart Automotive Campus, my thank you to you all from the bottom of my heart. My absence in mind and in person over these past six years has given me peace, especially during these times of loss, because you have carried the burden and done it so well. The original Playground Director, Wayne Elhart, would be very proud . . . in fact, you know he is!

Kindness

To the kind, friendly, generous, and considerate folks who helped me along the way in helping bring mental illness awareness and suicide prevention education to the West Michigan area, the state of Michigan, and our nation, a great big thank you. Thank you to the friends of the Wayne Elhart **be nice.** Memorial Fund. Thanks to your support, the **be nice.** program and action plan will continue beyond our time. Thank you to my agent Chip Brown and Proper Media. Your patience working with a first-time writer of a published book is so appreciated, and your mentorship helped me persevere to bring this book to fruition. Also, many thanks to Chris Tiegreen, my writer, who took my words and painted them into a road map, collage, and masterpiece for making this an applicable tool to help so many of all ages and backgrounds. Thank you to the many sources of information and data to support our work in this book that provides science to this learning experience. Finally, a special thank you to my seventh-grade English teacher, Steven Van Grouw, who inspired me to write and honored me some twenty-five years later by hand delivering to me my seventh-grade autobiography assignment, stating that my dreams for my future were remarkably met in his eyes.

Goodness

It's the small acts of goodness that our friends unselfishly do for me and our family that make me a better person. When our good friends notice how I am doing and stop and ask me, "Are you okay?" I know that I am loved and I matter. Thank you to all of my dear friends, from near and far; you are many.

Faithfulness

Faithfulness comes from a place of trust and loyalty. For that, I wish to especially thank Christ Fellowship Church of Palm Beach Gardens, Florida, where my brother Wayne recommitted his life to his Lord and Savior on December 7, 2014. Cherie and I love CFC and are happy to call you home! I would also like to thank Saddleback Church in Southern California for their Daily Hope Devotionals that have continually filled my spirit while grieving my brother's loss.

Gentleness

Thank you to the pastors in my life: Jonathan Brownson, Jim Liske, Mike Pitsenberger, Todd and Julie Mullins, Kay and Rick Warren, and Ben Aguilar. Thank you for helping lead me down the path of righteousness and eternal love and life. And thank you for embracing this topic in your continued life in leading God's kingdom.

Self-Control

A special thanks to those who helped me with my self-control, supported my knowledge or lack thereof in my emotions and desires and expression of them in my behavior. I have had the privilege of working with some special people who have helped me along the way in my own grief and funneling my emotions accordingly. Thank you to Dr. James Dumerauf, Dr. David Litts, Sheila Bauer, Dr. Jerry Reed, and the National Action Alliance for Suicide Prevention Executive Committee.

upstream prevention
through mental health education

be nice. equips individuals to recognize changes at the onset of an illness. This is an an upstream approach.

be nice. is a mental health and suicide prevention program that has an action plan. When used effectively, the **be nice.** program encourages individuals to challenge themselves and others to seek appropriate professional help when they notice changes in their mental health.

We are creating psychologically safe communities by:

- **EDUCATING** individuals of all ages to recognize the signs of mental illness and have the confidence to take action when helping themselves or others.

- **EDUCATING** communities to support the mental, emotional, and behavioral health of all individuals.

- **EDUCATING** individuals to reduce the shame, stigma, and secrecy surrounding mental illnesses and treatment so less people struggle silently and more people seek help.

- **EDUCATING** individuals about the warning signs of suicide and equipping them with the tools to act when someone is in crisis.

Visit: benice.org

be nice. deemed to be best practice.

Results from an evidenced based study conducted with Grand Valley State University show:

- Increases mental health awareness and resources available among staff, students, and parents
- Decreases the number of behavioral referrals and bullying incidents
- Provides a common language to discuss negative behaviors
- Increase in suicide prevention behaviors
- Improves climate and connectedness while increasing positive behaviors
- Integrates well with other character and behavioral school based programs
- Identified top-down support as most effective for successful implementation
- Sustainable with training and support provided by the Mental Health Foundation of West Michigan

a common language

education for all ages

confidence to take action when it comes to mental health

a sustainable program

community level awareness

Visit: benice.org

be nice. Programming

be nice. Business is a sustainable programming model utilizing business liaisons through a train-the-trainer method. A company's **be nice.** liaison will use the trainings and materials to bring the action plan to the work environment - helping to cultivate a psychologically safe work environment. For businesses of any size!

Visit: benicebusiness.org

be nice. Schools is an evidence-based, K-12 systematic approach to behavioral and mental health education and awareness. The **be nice.** program is a district-wide initiative to be implemented year after year. Repetition creates familiarity making the **be nice.** action plan common language. The goal is for students, school and support staff, and families to feel comfortable talking openly and honestly about mental health. It's proven that **be nice.** students are more apt to utilize resources if they are struggling or let a trusted adult know if they're worried about a friend. Once your school has successfully launched the first year of programming, **be nice.** chapters renew their membership each year to have continued access to new tools and supplies for sustaining the program.

Visit: beniceschools.org

be nice. Faith trains liaisons from faith communities to use create movement for mental health throughout their congregation. The **be nice.** action plan is a tool for the larger community to increase positive understanding of mental health, as well as a tool in one-on-one conversations. For some, faith is the number one protective factor in mental health - make sure that your faith community is prepared with the tools to begin these conversations about mental health, and empower members with resources, hope, and understanding.

Visit: benicefaith.org

be nice. Community: Whether educating groups of organizations on the **be nice.** action plan for mental health and suicide prevention, or hosting stigma reducing events, **be nice.** community helps to cultivate connectedness and ultimately, improves, changes, and saves lives.

Visit: benice.org